Taking Root to Fly

Articles on
Functional Anatomy

by Irene Dowd

Fourth Printing, 2001

This third revised edition, published by Irene Dowd in 1995, is a revised and expanded republication, with regard to both text and illustrations. The first edition 1981 and second edition 1990, were published by Irene Dowd in conjunction with Contact Editions, A project of Contact Collaborations, Inc.

Back cover photograph by Liza Matthews

Cover design by Charles Stokes

Designed and produced by G & H SOHO, Inc.

Earlier versions of the articles in this book previously appeared in the following magazines: *Eddy, Dance Scope,* and *Contact Quarterly.*

ISBN 0-9645805-0-0

Preface

to the Third Edition of Taking Root To Fly

The first edition of *Taking Root to Fly* reflected the profound influence of my teacher, Dr. Lulu E. Sweigard. The second edition revealed some of my thinking and dreaming about metaphoric pathways through the human body. This third edition is shaped by the effects on myself of seeing and touching my own students as they performed the movements of their daily lives over the years. Those choreographies of daily life ranged from word processing to playing the cello, walking to skiing, talking to singing, and mostly dancing, dancing, dancing; from ballet to postmodern.

Many of the understandings I have gained come from thinking of my students as "teachers," and taking "instruction" from the direct communication of their movement patterns to me through my touching fingers. While watching someone move, I also let myself minutely mirror that choreography within my own body so as to engage my own kinesthesia (sense of movement as perceived by one's own joints and muscles). By using my touch and vision in this way, I construct a sense of the individual kinesthetic anatomy particular to each person I come in contact with.

The addition of a new final article to this book describes some of the ways in which I actually perceive the persons I see and touch. "Metaphors of Touch" (1995) is a distillation of some of the elements included in four articles that were sensitively edited by Nancy Stark Smith and Lisa Nelson for publication in *Contact Quarterly*—"The Use of Intentional Touch" (1990), "Neutralization: Preparing for the

Intentional Touch Interaction" (1991), "Modes of Perception: Finding Pathways through Inner Worlds" (1992), and "Creating Motion through Intentional Touch" (1994).

When I reviewed the text and illustrations in the past editions of *Taking Root to Fly* from my present perspective, I could not resist making changes. The revised articles have been added to and elaborated in such a way as to make "Ideokinesis: The 9 Lines of Movement" (1983) redundant. Therefore, I have removed it from the third edition. An annotated bibliography has been added. I hope that the reader of this volume finds the descriptions and visual examples I have now created to be more varied, lucid, and dynamic.

Irene Dowd
February 1995

Preface
to the Second Edition of
Taking Root To Fly

The ten articles included in this new edition of *Taking Root To Fly* span ten years. "On Breathing" was first published in 1976 and "In Honor of the Foot" appeared in 1986. In retrospect, I see the early pieces—"On Breathing" (1976), "Finding Your Center" (1977), and "Standing on Two Legs" (1978)—as concerning themselves with the anatomical differences between humans and animals and the way in which our skeleton embodies human aspirations. Like my teacher, Lulu Sweigard, I was fascinated by the desire of humans to thrust upward from earth to sky in ardent vertical simplicity, and the need to move from a central core of self in order to feel powerful in the world.

The middle articles—"Enfolding and Exposing" (1978), "Visualizing Movement Potential" (1979), "The Dark Side of the Brain" (1980), and "Taking Root to Fly" (1980)—came from explorations of the fantastic and whimsical power of metaphor in my own life. "Ideokinesis" (1983) marks the beginning of a shift from focus within the body to a broader sphere of action beyond the body boundaries. I began to be more concerned with variations in function from one individual to another.

In the last articles—"On Metaphor" (1984) and "In Honor of the Foot" (1986)—my interest became somewhat more "environmental." Here I began to address the complex variability and possibility of interaction between world and the self living in that world.

Irene Dowd
June 1990

Contents

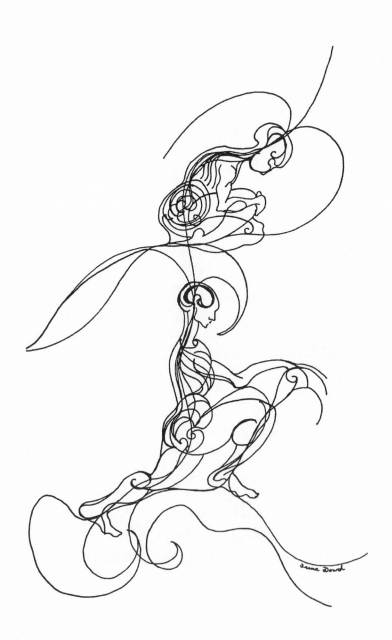

Visualizing Movement Potential

I had a notebook filled with unanswered questions when Dr. Lulu Sweigard* died. Over the six years that I studied with her and assisted her "Anatomy for Dancers" class in the Juilliard School, she repeated some things so many times that I can still hear them echoing. Nonetheless, I was now terrified that I could never go back to her again to ask about real-life students whose bodies refused to fit into any of the neat categories of size, shape, or movement that I knew. It was a long time before I understood that the often-repeated words were themselves guidelines for reasoning out the answers to all the "new" questions and problems I found.

There were two main principles she established to use in aiding the performance of movement: the essence of dance and life itself. The first is that all postural alignment patterns, all muscle use and development, all human body movement is directed and coordinated by the activity of our nervous system, in other words, our thinking. Therefore, in order to change our body shape or our movement patterns we must change our neurological activity. Although most of

*Dr. Lulu E. Sweigard (Ph. D., New York University) is the author of *Human Movement Potential: Its Ideokinetic Facilitation,* a widely used reference for motor learning and dance educators. The book came out of her extensive scientific research at New York University and many years of experience as a teacher of movement at New York University, Columbia University, and finally the Juilliard School where she spent the last decades of her life working with dancers.

this neurological activity is habitual and/or nonconscious, changing our exact conscious goals affects this extensive subcortical, unconscious process.

The second principle is that "dis-ease," joint and muscle pain, and limited movement range and vocabulary are all products of imbalance. The human body, being an unstable structure, is constantly in motion, constantly vibrating like a tuning fork around the point of mechanical balance but never settling fixedly upon it. The more closely the body approaches this balancing point, the greater the balance of muscle action around joints. This minimizes the stress on the joints and ligaments and lessens the possibility of chronic pain or injury. If the muscles around the joint are all working in a balanced way, none of them is constantly contracted and none is constantly at rest. Their alternating rhythmical activity serves an important function in pumping blood through the body and maintaining flexibility and strength. When there is poor balance so that weight is not transferred through the centers of joints, some of the muscles must contract continuously to counteract the pull of gravity. This limits our movement range because a constantly contracted muscle is both a fatigued muscle and an inflexible one. Other muscles may be constantly relaxed, resulting in excessively unstable joints and rapid fatigue when movement is performed.

Both of these principles seem obvious. After all, we act on them continuously if not consciously. The way in which Dr. Sweigard applied them, however, was uncompromising and sophisticated, and not at all obvious to me even after years of experiencing the dramatic effect of their application to my own body. She sought the way to bring a balance of flexibility and strength to all of the muscles of the body, twenty-four hours a day, no matter what the person's activity. To accomplish this aim, she taught people to visualize lines of movement traveling through their bodies, at first while they were lying down in what she called the constructive rest position, and then later while they were standing and moving about at their normal activities. These lines of movement had specific locations and directional pathways through the body that were based on the skeletal structure and muscular functions of the individual she was working with at the time.

Visualizing a line of movement through the body while not moving can change the habitual patterns of messages being sent from the brain through nerve pathways to the muscles. As long as this new thinking pattern is activated during movement, a new pattern of muscle activity is automatically being used to decrease physical stress and maintain a more balanced alignment of skeletal parts. Over a period of time during which there is continual daily attention to new habit patterns in thinking and action, the body's shape will be transformed. Previously overused muscles become more flexible and smoothed out, while previously underused muscles develop greater tone, strength, endurance, and a fuller contour.

When Dr. Sweigard used the term "movement goal," she had something very precise in mind: what you want to be doing right now. Long-term goals are a direction to follow, perhaps a philosophy or dream life. If your greatest aim is to be able to fly you will have to construct a step-by-step series of short-term goals to achieve that end. Each short-term goal must be something within your capability so that you can actually visualize yourself doing it and then actually do it. Begin with walking. If you can do this, it will give you positive reinforcement to take on the next more difficult goal. If walking is beyond your capacity, don't keep failing. Not even a worm will persist after repeated negative reinforcement. The solution is to go one step back to something you can do, crawling perhaps. By keeping your current movement goal at a level of possible attainment, you will be ready to go beyond it with success. If you are in pain, whether you are moving or not, your most compelling immediate goal is to get rid of the hurt. The next essential goal is to be able to move fully without getting into pain again.

One condition that seems to be a prerequisite for chronic pain is a habitual imbalance of muscle usage around a particular joint or joints. Some of the muscles crossing a joint are weaker than others, some are stronger. There is a situation of relative weakness but not of absolute weakness. Your own muscles have to counteract each other in order to cause movement. Furthermore, if weight is habitually never transferred through the center of a joint, some of the muscles that cross the joint are constantly being stretched while others are more contracted and unable to stretch nearly as much. Stronger muscles may be more massive than weaker ones, but if they are too massive they get in the way of full movement range. Depending on the relationship of the joint to the line of gravity, some muscles may be working to counteract the force of gravity almost continually and will therefore have great endurance. Muscles which are not functioning to hold the bone upright or initiate movement may become so weak that they are difficult to engage and have almost no ability to endure.

To complicate matters even more, there are three kinds of muscle contraction. A muscle can contract and shorten to cause movement at a joint (concentric contraction). This happens in the muscles across the front of the hip joint as you flex to bring your leg up in front of you. A muscle can contract and neither shorten nor lengthen, as when you are holding your leg up in the air for a while (isometric contraction). A muscle can also contract and lengthen, which is what happens in the muscles across the front of the hip joint as you gradually lower your leg back to the floor (eccentric contraction). Practicing one kind of contraction enables you to do more of just that kind, but it doesn't help you with the other two kinds. In other words, what you practice is what you can do. There is no one all-around exercise that prepares you for everything else.

Even if you have a perfectly centered alignment and exceedingly pleasing contours with totally even muscle action around all the joints, holding yourself rigidly in this position may result in severe pain. You will certainly be unable to move freely. This is because all the muscles are constantly doing an isometric contraction. If you do not practice the two other kinds of contraction in your daily life, the joint or joints around which the muscles are tightly contracted may eventually feel stiff.

Clearly, the imbalance at a joint that is "out of line" does not just involve muscle weakness. It involves a relative imbalance in mass, endurance, and flexibility as well as strength. If a joint is being held in "perfect alignment," all the muscles are contracting just to hold you up and are therefore at a great disadvantage when called on to make you move. Once we begin to move, of course, one of the major determinants of our ability to please ourselves and those who see us is our skill in coordinating the patterns of stretch and contraction of our muscles. A person with strong, flexible, enduring muscles may make a lovely statue, but without skilled timing, this same person will be a hopelessly awkward and vulnerable dancer.

Determining which abilities an injured muscle lacks or has in excess abundance is not simple. The likelihood of finding a single exercise that performed three times daily will cure us is very very slight. When even a single muscle or ligament is injured, the whole body compensates for its temporary weakness. Once the injury is healed, the whole body has to readjust so that the now whole part is not still favored and thereby further weakened by misuse or even non-use. Indeed, there is often a tendency to favor a particular body part before the injury. The injury only reinforces this habit pattern. Once an injured muscle is healed, it is inevitably a little weaker, less flexible, less enduring, and even smaller than the other muscles that were still functioning while it was hurt. For this reason, one cannot immediately go back to making the same demands on it that one made before. One must gradually retrain it in all its functions if one does not want to run the risk of maintaining the idiosyncratic movement patterns of pain. This is, of course, a new training—learning to use the muscle more effectively than before the injury.

Before I set up a program of movement practice for anyone, I make clear to myself and the student that it is a teaching-learning process. Dr. Sweigard never tired of telling me, to her very last days, that she and I were teachers, not doctors, not therapists, not healers. She reminded me and showed me again and again that the work of a teacher is to give students the tools of knowledge and skills to help themselves change their own patterns of movement. The good teacher gives the student the ability to be self-responsible. Effective teachers make themselves obsolete in the end.

The task of teachers of movement is not diagnosing structural pathology and medically treating it. Our task is seeing how the structure functions and giving the understanding and useful tools to our students to perform movement more and more effectively so that in the process they themselves remove the habits that cause pathology.

A student who is in real pain should first be sent for a thorough medical examination to rule out any possibility of disease, endocrine imbalance, acute injury, or any other type of problem that requires medical treatment. Once it is clear that the student's problem stems from the way the body is being used I feel free to step in and offer new movement patterns.

After obtaining a general history of the student, both medical and personal, I would first examine that person's basic skeletal alignment patterns and muscle structure when standing erect, sitting, lying down, and finally "folded-over" so that the entire spine was flexed. Sometimes this process alone would lead me to identify elements of the student's problem and an approach to the solution. Often, however, especially when I first began my apprenticeship with Dr. Sweigard, my examination would only leave me baffled. Whenever I went to Dr. Sweigard to question her about the nature of my student's problems, she would inevitably ask "Did you look at movement?"

No matter how curious the student's muscular or skeletal structure seemed to me, if I paid close enough attention long enough to the way in which the person moved this structure, I could eventually discover the nature of the problem and the tools for solving it. Sometimes, especially in the beginning when my eye was not attuned to subtle movement functions, I would have to watch students perform daily activities not just self-consciously before me, but also in their normal setting. Sometimes it was necessary for me to see them taking a strenuous dance class at the studio where they were on scholarship or performing on stage where adrenaline freed their usual physical inhibitions.

Occasionally, what seemed at first like a problem of chronic muscular tension or weakness when I observed the student at rest gave evidence of a medical problem as I viewed the person in action over a period of time. One student was very tense, but his movement patterns didn't seem to warrant the excruciating headaches he suffered daily. It turned out that he had a brain tumor that required surgery. Another student who had satisfactorily recovered from a bad knee injury was practicing all the movements that I gave her correctly and faithfully every day for months. Nonetheless, her muscles were not getting any stronger; in fact there were signs of atrophy. At last I questioned her thoroughly about her life style and discovered that she was suffering from protein deficiency.

Fortunately, these sorts of cases are rare, but they taught me a lesson: that I have the capacity and training to work with imbalances in movement and alignment patterns only. While such imbalances are responsible for a whole host of symptoms, they are not the cause of all ills. These others are beyond my ken. The best that each of us can do is know our strongest abilities and develop them fully while recognizing our limitations. Saying "I don't know" when we really don't is essential if we want to avoid injuring ourselves and the people we work with.

Whatever the nature of the skeletal deviations and resultant muscle imbalances practiced by the student which accompany low back stiffness, for example, having the person "think toward center," as Dr. Sweigard used to say, will aid the individual. The trick, of course, is to get the student to "think center" in the right location and direction without forcing movement and without losing concentration, even under the most pressured or emotional circumstances. Eventually one must succeed in finding a way for the student to be at ease in the low back not just when lying still but also while performing a full range of movement in the lumbar spine.

The student must start working in a position where it is not necessary to deal with gravity at all, much less fight it. The obvious position is lying down. I like to work with a slight variation of the supine position which Dr. Sweigard called the constructive rest position (CRP). In this position the person is lying on the back with arms at ease and legs bent so that the feet stand onto the floor while the knees point to the ceiling. [fig. 1] The feet can be braced against a wall or a cushion and the knees can be tied together with a sash so that no work is required to keep the legs in position. An alternative

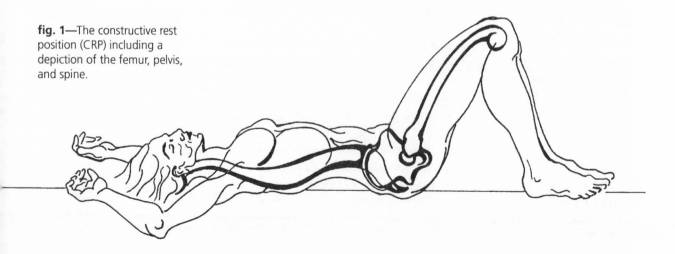

fig. 1—The constructive rest position (CRP) including a depiction of the femur, pelvis, and spine.

is to rest the legs on a chair seat or stool. The reason for assuming this position rather than one in which the legs are extended out along the floor is that in the latter position the pelvis is tipped downward in front while the lumbar spine is hyperextended because of the pull of the tight ileofemoral ligament that crosses the front of the hip joint. When there is already discomfort in the low back area, an exaggerated arching of the lumbar spine is hardly desirable. In CRP the lower back is slightly off the floor, just enough so that you can slip the palm of your hand in the space between it and the floor. Flattening the back completely against the floor is just as much of a spinal distortion as overarching it. Both can cause pain and involve excess muscle work even though you may not feel it.

What follows is the "script" of a hypothetical session in neuromuscular coordination with a student who has low back stiffness, not due to a medical problem.

The first act in this supine position is nonaction. In CRP it is hypothetically possible to completely stop working, so as to give up previously learned habits that you want to replace with more functional ones. This may be an extremely difficult undertaking for you. Very often it is the inability to stop doing that creates major physical problems in the first place. There are a number of ways to stop doing. Check your body in its entirety, allowing yourself to be fully supported by the ground beneath you. You may think of every part of your body as being fluid, like sand or water, flowing outward and downward into the ground. If this doesn't work easily, try tensing each part of your body as hard as you can and then releasing all effort in that part completely. Go through every part of your body beginning with your head and moving on down through to your toes. If you have gone too quickly through this process, you will not have interrupted your state of extreme muscular control. Return to your head once more and let yourself gradually begin emptying or clearing yourself by visualizing movement along internal pathways. Your preliminary goal is to relax the muscles of facial expression, which in turn facilitates the concentration required to proceed.

First, visualize your skull as being a large and airy, totally empty room. Scan with your mind's eye (not your physical eyes) from the base of your skull where your neck meets your scalp, along the smooth expanse of space within your head, all the way over your forehead to your eyebrows. If your skull isn't quite empty, repeat the process of scanning again, sweeping its vast space clear this time. When you get to the center of your forehead, between your eyebrows, visualize all the unnecessary contents of your head, like breath or water, flowing out along your eyebrows to melt off into the ground. Visualize likewise a flow outward from your nose, along your cheek bones to your ears. Let all the excess drip from your ears to the ground. The sockets for your eyes are very large and deep. Let your gently closed (not squeezed shut) eyes expand and fill the entire space of their sockets. Perhaps your eye sockets can enlarge even more. Don't try to see the space with your eyes. Just allow them to expand gently and rest in the dark cool pools of space that grow softly in your head. Sometimes lightly resting your palms over your eyes so that your hands keep out the light allows the eyes to rest more easily. In the absence of light the eyes do not need to strain to see.

Place your fingertips on your jaw joints on either side of your head, just in front of your ears. Move your jaw a little to locate the exact place. Now think of there being space in the joint between the two articulating bones. Visualize your fingertips sinking through the space so that your hands move softly towards each other. Let your fingertips glide easily downward to your chin until they actually meet. Think of the bones beneath your fingers flowing with them.

There is a lot of space within the cavern of the mouth. With each breath you exhale, think that the air passing through your throat and into the cavern of your mouth enlarges the space within just as underground rivers wear away subterranean caves into vast hallways and rooms. Allow the exhale phase of your breathing to be long and lazy, circulating around the base of your tongue, creating eddies in all the echo chambers, exploring and expanding your inner space as air effortlessly seeps out of you. Simply attending to the exhale phase of breathing is sometimes all that is needed to give up excessive muscular controls or obsessive and distracting mental activity. Let what you don't want matter-of-factly flow out of you along with the air you exhale.

Cup your hands over your ears so that your fingertips are touching lightly around your ears but you are not pressing on the ears themselves. Visualize your ears expanding like the concentric circles of ripples in a pond when a pebble is dropped in it. You can think of the ears rotating as they expand like a pinwheel or a spiral nebula. Because there are so many muscles of skull and neck attaching all around the ears, imagining the ears "relaxing" or opening like budding flowers affects all these simultaneously. Once these muscles release their hold, the head may rest without any work at all, perfectly balancing on the top of the spine (the mid-point of a line extending through the head from ear to ear locates the place where the head sits on top of the spine).

Finally, let your fingertips rest on the bulges just below your ears. These are the mastoid bones, which serve as the attachments of the sternocleidomastoid muscles, a pair of muscles that are often tight in anyone who has a forward head or chin. Think of your fingertips melting right through your neck and meeting at center. Let your fingers move down your neck to your collar bones and think of all the excess energy, no longer being contained as muscle tension, flowing out your shoulders, through your arms and out your fingertips like beams of light.

You may feel quite pleasurable sensations. If so, enjoy them but do not be distracted by them. They are only side effects of achieving your goal. Now that your head is cleared of distraction, the "internal dialogue" interrupted, you can begin to think with new, positively focused direction into the area that has perhaps been a source of limitation or pain in the past. Do not think about the unpleasant sensations which you may have previously associated with the low back or pelvis, for example. Instead allow the space you have created in your now clear and focused mind to flow like water or air or light down through your trunk to create even more room within your body. Expand to your full size on the ground like a lake that cannot help but fill its basin.

Each time you inhale, you might think of your breath expanding your spine (which it actually does) so that all the little tight-held places in your back melt outward and downward on to the ground that holds you. Each exhale may drain out the old soreness and tensions and debris along with the excess carbon dioxide. If it is easy for you to think of your breath without forcefully controlling its rate or depth, you can visualize it going more deeply into and through your body until your spine has grown long and free without any muscle action on your part. If, for any reason, you do not wish to think of your breath moving you, make up a new form of imagined activity which is both vivid and pleasurable to you. Any force you want to imagine can lengthen your spine by sinking your sacrum weightily toward your heels and shooting your central axis out the top of your head. Do not dwell on any kinks, twists, or knots in your spine. Simply let strong forces of energy act within you to ease your spine to its full length and width and depth without distortion. Allow your belly to release. Let your abdominal contents sink down with gravity, to rest on the front of your spine. Let these forces balance each other until you rest centered, vibrating around your central axis. [fig. 2]

Having allowed yourself to come to neutral, you are finally ready to perform any movement in your mind's eye. Do not rush to this

fig. 2—Lying in CRP visualizing the spine lengthening to send the sacrum toward the heels, the central axis growing out through the top of the head, and the abdominal contents sinking toward the front of the spine.

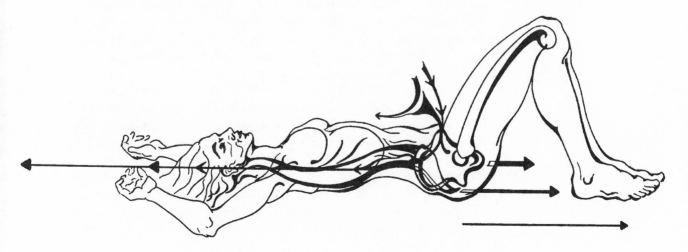

state of readiness. Being neutral or centered, euphemistically called "being relaxed," is the best preparation for any action, particularly a challenging one. More preparation than this only involves extra muscle work and strain. Obviously, it is impossible to concentrate on your movement goal if you are all tied up in preparing for it. In a state of receptive neutrality, it will be easiest for you to visualize the movement you wish to perform without any ineffectual old habits of muscle action, pain, and strain coming into play.

This next part is up to you. Start visualizing the simplest, most basic components of the more complex movement pattern you wish to achieve. For example, you might visualize performing easy arm or leg movements which leave your spine long and stable. Progress to actually flexing at the hip joint of one leg so that your leg swings easily off the ground without your pelvis having to shift or your spine distort. Perhaps you want to try making small circles of the thigh bone in the hip socket. Think of the movement as being frictionless in a well-lubricated and roomy joint. Try alternating legs and imagine that both move with the ease of the one that had previously been "the good leg." Perhaps you will allow your hands and arms to caress and sculpt the air. You might even try coordinating the movement of your arms and legs in opposition. Whatever small, rounded joint movements you perform, arcing your limbs through external space maintains all the internal space you found before. All the while, your mind's eye is traveling along the continuous length of your spine which grows more spacious even as you pass along it.

Warmed and made more fluid by your rhythmic swinging of arms and legs, rest quietly again for a moment. Maintaining your sense of energetic unity, visualize movement that is more difficult for you to perform in real space. If it has been a challenge to swing your leg behind you, now see it, in your mind's eye only, sweeping into the backward curve of an arabesque, spine arching effortlessly and evenly throughout its entire length. If you can picture the growth of a single curve from big toe to top of head, a flawless arabesque, move on to an arabesque turn or leaps through space, all the while seeing your spine as a whole, now spiralling as well as arcing. Practice visualizing any movement pattern you desire that you have found painful or difficult in actual physical performance but which you can now imagine with perfect clarity. Practice the movement in your mind until you can repeat it with the right tempo and dynamics and energy and dramatic intent, again and again. Without the interference of your habitual and less efficient patterns of action, it is possible to visualize perfection. In simply visualizing you are nonetheless activating the precise neurological pathways that may allow you to accomplish your full movement goal. You are actually establishing new habit patterns in your nervous system which can replace the old ones you no longer desire.

If at any time you notice that you are drawing your eyebrows together, clenching your teeth, gripping your back, pulling your shoulder blades together, grabbing in your buttocks, etc. simply go through the process which brings you back to neutral. Do not keep practicing your imagined action until you have given up your wasteful physical effort. Otherwise you will just be further reinforcing undesirable habits before you even stand up.

No matter how slowly you have had to proceed through your internal adventures, it is never a good idea to remain immobile in one position for very long. There is little reason to stay supine for more than about twenty minutes at a time. Even if you have not finished going through the process you should get up after twenty minutes. There is always time to finish later in the day or tomorrow. Too lengthy a practice, physical or mental, tends eventually to prove counterproductive, since our patterns of movement and thought when we are fatigued are not always our most efficient ones. Conversely, more frequent shorter practices may speed the training process. It is also true that serious injuries often take place when strenuous practice has gone on too long and the participants are fatigued. While you are unlikely to injure yourself in CRP, you are also unlikely to be working constructively when you are exhausted or bored.

Once you have gotten up, stand quietly for a moment or two and see if you can allow head, rib cage, and pelvis to be centered in relation to each other and effortlessly supported and connected by your spine. Let your sacrum hang down to connect you to the ground just behind your heels. Let your central axis, soaring out through the top of your head, suspend you from the sky.

Stable and yieldingly tall, warm yourself up gradually by doing small, fluid, rhythmic whole body movements which gradually increase in their range and speed. When you have lubricated and heated all your joints with easy activity, begin performing the movements which are most basic and of little technical challenge to you, move along through to the most difficult and complex ones. You will probably find that at least the very first movement you perform will be surprisingly easy and full. Make sure that you really start with the most basic movement elements: walking before leaping. Congratulate yourself on each success no matter how small it seems. If you couldn't do it as well before, you have progressed. Repeat the successful movement until it feels "natural" and predictable instead of "weird" and accidental. Repeated daily practice until you get "the feel of the movement" not only reinforces the necessary neurological patterns but also starts to develop your muscles in the necessary way to produce the patterns.

If you find that the movement you are performing is no longer successful, STOP! Do not keep practicing a pattern that is nonfunctional. This might only train you to fail more consistently in the future. Instead, pause and clear your mind of everything. Return to neutral and then visualize the perfect execution of the movement pattern that you want to achieve. Now you are ready to perform the movement again. If you continue to fail, you have either skipped the practice of an essential intermediate, simpler pattern of action or you have reached your limits for the moment. If there is a more basic pattern that you need to practice, turn your attention to performing it. Only after you have mastered it should you return to the more complex activity. On the other hand, if you have reached your limit for now, quit. Take a break. Either your muscles are fatigued by new and unusual usage not required by your old habits of action, or else you are mentally fatigued by an unfamiliar intensity or duration of concentration.

It is time to do something totally different and unrelated. Don't even think about what you have just been doing. Forget it entirely until your next practice session which can be a little later in the day or the next day. If you practice too infrequently, the next time will take you back almost to your starting point, severely slowing your progress in neuromuscular conditioning.

Do not expect your next session to begin with a perfectly transformed body. While it is true that you are changing constantly, the changes that take place from day to day are extremely subtle. It takes about two months of daily practice from the time you have started to think about your movement differently to the time that your muscles visibly change shape. While sixty days into the future seems like a long time to wait before a new internal balance brings tangible results, it isn't very long at all in comparison to your whole life, which you have already spent developing the form you now have.

Remember also that not even the greatest teacher can speed the process of change or do it for you. What someone says or writes or shows you can draw your attention to aspects of your movement which can be improved and can spark your imagination with appropriate imagery. But it is your sustained concentration on your own balance of energy usage, visible and invisible, that will move you to achievement of your full movement potential. There is no "right image" or "right posture" or even "right movement." There is only a way of functioning that is both unifying and expansive for you at this moment. Furthermore, this way of functioning will change continuously throughout life. Plasticity of mind is what makes movement possible at all. If you can conceive of the human body doing a particular movement, then you can learn to do it. The miracle is that you don't fall down in shock when you find yourself doing it, every cell moving in perfect harmony, no room for a tiny knot that says, "I can't."

2

On Breathing

Anyone who has ever pursued a physical discipline has been made aware of breathing, either by his or her own body or by the instructions of a teacher. Each of us has learned that while breath is essential for life and is completely automatic (you can't commit suicide by holding your breath because after a certain point you pass out and start breathing in spite of your will), it can nonetheless be altered in a wide variety of ways. Not only can breath be speeded up or slowed down, counted, held in or held out, but it can also feel like it is being initiated in different parts of the body. Often a dance student can become terribly confused, and out of breath, when one teacher suggests, "hold your chest high as if you were inhaling," while another says, "keep your ribs down so that your chest doesn't move when you breathe." Any new breathing technique seems to work well at first although the dancer may eventually find that his or her endurance is decreasing in the long run when trying to do only "abdominal" breathing or "hold the stomach in" and do only "chest" breathing. Fortunately, most of us don't pay any attention at all to our breathing when we are dancing strenuously so that the wisdom of our body takes over.

Perhaps a brief description of what happens under the surface when we breathe can help us make sense out of all the helpful hints we get about breathing. Our torso is divided into two main sections: the thoracic cavity and the abdominal cavity. The thoracic cavity includes everything contained in the rib cage which extends from

13

fig. 1—A schematic representation of the side view of the human trunk. The lined area represents the thoracic cavity, the crosshatched area the abdominal cavity, and the black area between the two cavities represents the diaphragm in a released (uncontracted) position. The arrows indicate that as the diaphragm contracts on an inhalation, the thoracic cavity floor will move down, causing the roof of the abdominal cavity to be lowered so that the abdominal contents will press outward toward the front of the trunk and downward into the pelvis.

the base of the neck to a few inches above the navel. Essentially, it is a sealed-off container for the lungs, with the heart resting in between. The abdominal cavity consists of the part of the trunk that begins at the lower border of the rib cage and fills the space down into the pelvis. This sack contains the digestive organs. The two cavities are separated by a thin strong muscle called the diaphragm. It attaches all around the lower border of the rib cage and ties down to the lower spine in back. It is like a hemisphere that arches up into the thoracic cavity forming both the roof of the abdominal cavity and the floor of the thoracic cavity.

During inhalation, the thoracic cavity must be enlarged so that air can rush into the lungs. The thoracic cavity can be increased in size by expanding the rib cage upward and outward to increase the circumference of the cavity. This increase is caused by the contraction of the muscles between the ribs, called the intercostal muscles. In the case of an extraordinarily large inhalation, muscles from the shoulders and the top of the rib cage going up to attach on the neck and skull can also contract to lift the rib cage even higher. Each rib attaches to the spine in the back of the trunk so that as we inhale, each rib can move upward and out from the spine. This means that while the rib cage tends to move as a whole, we can move segments of it in isolation. It also means that when the rib cage expands, we can see the movement around the entire trunk, in back as well as in front. The thoracic cavity is further increased by lowering its floor, in other words, by contracting the diaphragm so that it does not bulge up as far into the thoracic cavity. When the diaphragm contracts, it flattens downward to press on the top of the abdominal cavity. This increases the pressure in the abdomen causing the "stomach to stick out" if one is not contracting the abdominal muscles. Diaphragm contraction also results in a sensation of increasing pressure down into the pelvis if the abdominal muscles are contracting to maintain the "flat stomach." Because of the effect of the diaphragm on the abdomen, use of the diaphragm is called "belly" or "abdominal" breathing.[fig. 1]

During exhalation, the decrease in size of the thoracic cavity happens through a reversal of the above process. The muscles between the ribs and in the upper chest elongate, allowing the rib cage to narrow and drop due to the downward pull of gravity on the ribs. The diaphragm rises back up into the thoracic cavity as it is drawn there by the natural elasticity of the lungs to which it clings. The result is a decrease in the circumference and depth of the thoracic cavity which forces air out of the lungs as they are pressed flatter. For this reason, breathing moderately deeply, with particular attention to the exhalation, is an excellent and simple method of generally easing the neck, shoulder, and back areas.[fig. 2]

At this point it is easy to understand why the whole trunk either

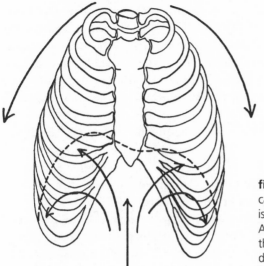

fig. 2—Front view of the rib cage. The top of the diaphragm is shown with a dotted line. Arrows indicate the motions of the rib cage and the diaphragm during the exhalation phase of breathing.

moves or experiences a change of pressure as one inhales and exhales. In order to achieve an optimum oxygen intake, expand the ribs as fully as possible without contracting the muscles of the neck so as not to constrict the passageway for the air from the nose to the lungs and inhibit the flow of air to them. At the same time contract the diaphragm as fully as possible without overly distorting the abdominal wall in the front of the trunk. Exhale as fully as possible without adding excess muscular effort since the more muscles used in contracting, the more rapidly is the supply of oxygen used.

It is important to passively let out as much air as possible since the amount of air left in the lungs from a previous inhalation limits the amount of fresh air that can be taken in during the next inhalation. The fresh air taken in has a higher level of necessary oxygen than the residual air left in the lungs, and the residual air has a higher level of carbon dioxide and other waste products from muscle and cellular metabolism. Thus it is easy to see that the body can function for a longer period of time at a level of high activity if as much air as possible is expelled after taking in as much fresh air as possible.

It becomes clear that much of the valuable advice on breathing given us is quite useful as long as it is all used simultaneously. Oxygen intake is increased when we use "chest breathing" as well as "abdominal breathing," breathing "from the back," "from the pelvis," and indeed "through the whole trunk." However, anyone who has tried to think of five things at once while executing a series of rapid and complicated dance steps knows that such experiments end at least in frustration and possibly painful accidents. If we think about our breathing at all when we are dancing, we must have one single thought or image in mind that we can hold constant as we move. One unifying idea is imagining the breath going up and down the central axis of the body which extends from between the hip joints up through the pelvis, the center of the neck, between the ears, and on to the top of the head. One thinks of the breath just passing up and down this axis or pole continually neither controlling the breath rate nor bypassing any part of the length of the pole.

You can imagine your central axis acquiring "thickness" until it is a cylinder with a circumference expanded enough to encompass your whole trunk. Think of it expanding in all directions simultaneously as you inhale and shrinking simultaneously in all directions as you exhale so that it collapses around its core.

Many of us tend to automatically put too much or too little emphasis on various parts of our trunk when we breathe. One person may tend to squeeze the ribs down and close the throat so that the belly alone puffs out. Another person might tend to hold the rib cage high at all times so that the neck partially disappears even when he or she is exhaling. Both of these tendencies, often noticeable in dancers, decrease the oxygen potential and add unnecessary tension to the body.

If you are aware of "puffing out" a particular part of your body when you inhale, just watch your breath flow past that area through the very center of your trunk without getting stuck. Don't try to "suck in" a part that bulges out when you inhale as this will only increase your tension, but simply allow that part to be soft, deflated, and empty. Let it be fluid. In your mind's eye, see the air go past it rather than filling it. In the areas where you feel that you "squeeze down" or have "knots," watch the air flow by like a stream of water, to soften and dissolve them.

Paying attention to your breathing without controlling it requires a high degree of concentration. It is easiest to do when you don't have to deal with gravity as well. You might start watching your breathing while lying on your back. If you have a very deep chest and lying in this position throws your head back and your chin up in the air, you can put a small pillow or pad under your head, not your neck.

My favorite imagery for enhancing coordinated "chest" (costal) and "belly" (diaphragmatic) breathing comes from one of my colleagues, Lynn Martin, a specialist in breathing mechanics. I imagine that my trunk is a composite of two domed cylinders, one sitting above the other. The top cylinder is composed of my rib cage and thoracic vertebrae. The bottom cylinder, which fits part way up into the top cylinder, is composed of the diaphragm as its dome-top, the abdominal wall muscles as its walls, and the bony pelvis as its base. As I inhale, the top cylinder will rise slightly upward and simultaneously expand outward so that its circumference increases. Meanwhile, the bottom cylinder's dome-shaped roof will lower as its walls expand outward to increase its circumference and firmly ground the bottom cylinder into the pelvic floor.

If I visualize the excursion upward and outward of the top cylinder during the inhalation, I will be increasing my costal breathing. If I visualize the excursion downward and outward of the bottom cylinder during the inhale, I will be increasing my diaphragmatic breathing. If I watch the two cylinders gently move apart at the very same instant, I am enhancing the coordination of all my respiratory muscles to increase the efficiency of my inhalation.

In order to sustain a longer and easier exhale, for speaking or singing, I imagine that the bottom cylinder begins to decrease its circumference at its base in the pelvis first so that it can then slowly rise up into the center of the top cylinder. After the bottom cylinder has begun to move upward at the beginning of the exhale, I imagine the top cylinder start to slowly and gently float down to rest ever so lightly above it. [fig. 3]

Do not attempt to control your rate or depth of breathing. When you are lying down quietly, your breath will automatically slow down and deepen without any effort on your part. Make sure you are really only thinking about the ideal flow of breath. Do not worry about or even think about what you believe to be your old, less efficient breathing patterns for you will only reinforce them by thinking about them. Don't think about how tense you are; only think about how the tension is dissolving with your breath flow.

If you find it difficult to allow a full exhalation or if you tend to force the air out of your lungs, think of your whole trunk as a big elas-

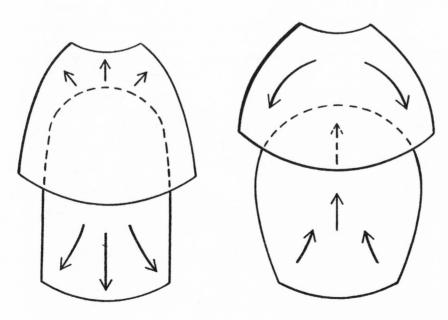

fig. 3—Representation of the trunk as two cylinders. The drawing on the left indicates the position of the two cylinders at the beginning of the inhalation. The arrows on this drawing show the directions in which the cylinders will move during the inhalation.

The drawing on the right indicates the position of the two cylinders at the beginning of the exhalation. The arrows on this second drawing show the directions in which the cylinders will move during the exhalation, be it silent or sung.

tic balloon whose natural elasticity expels the air out of your lungs when your wind pipe is open. Watch the balloon collapse all by itself to result in the flow of air out of your lungs. Actually allowing an "aaaah" or a "haa" sound to come out as you exhale can help. If the sound is clear, resonant and open, so is your chest and throat; if it is tight and high and jerky, go back to watching your center breathing and see if you can find the spot where the breath seems to be blocked. When you find it, just watch the breath flowing by, dissolving it and moving it out of you easily and gently with the sound. Make no effort at all to dissolve the block, just watch it flow away. If you can allow the making of sounds to give you pleasure, it is much easier to breathe fully and openly. Try playing with your breath. Be gentle and humorous. Laughter and lightness have a much greater effect on the dissipation of tension than hard, serious grasping and pushing.

When you are ready to get up, roll over on your side slowly. Using your hands to help you, stand up slowly so that your spine remains long and erect. Bend at your hip joints rather than in your spine to rise. Do not get up by raising your head and flexing your spine to create tension in your neck and distortion in your entire spine. Be careful not to jump up suddenly, since it may make you dizzy.

Once you are standing, allow yourself to continue breathing through your central axis. As you dance, your entire trunk will expand slightly in all directions as you inhale. This expansion will be almost imperceptible to someone watching, even if you take a rather deep breath, since it is distributed evenly around your central axis. For the same reason, a large inhalation will not undermine your balance even if you are balanced on one leg. As you exhale, your entire trunk will ease closer to your central axis, further enhancing the balance of your weight around a center core. As the central axis itself remains stable, there will be no sense of "collapse" as you exhale fully but only a sense of your body hanging lightly around it. Since your bones are more closely aligned around a central line, your muscles won't have to work as hard to hold you up against the pull of gravity.

You might now think of yourself as being like a pine tree whose trunk shoots up through its center growing always taller as the sap flows upward. At the same time, your outside—skin, arms, shoulders, ribs—hang all around you just as the tree's branches and leaves hang to move only in the wind, without effort.

Finding Your Center

The bony part of the human pelvis is shaped somewhat like a funnel that holds our centers of movement and creation. I will attempt to show how the structure of this part of our skeleton provides a stable base of support for powerful and wide-ranging movement when it is aligned as its design dictates in relation to the rest of the body.

Mechanically and functionally speaking, the pelvis is like the hub of a wheel. Within this circle of bone is the center of gravity of the human body, the point around which the entire body weight balances equally above and below, and to all sides. From this still point at the center of the wheel radiate the spokes of movement. In our bodies muscles connect the other skeletal parts of legs, spine, rib cage, arms and head to the pelvis so that movement can be initiated from our center. When the pelvis itself travels through space, just like the hub of a wheel, it carries the rest of the body along.

Three pelvic bones gird our center of gravity: the sacrum and the two os innominata (hip bones). The sacrum functions both as the end of the spine and as the back of the pelvic girdle. It is the bone closest to our center of gravity which is located just in front of the top of the sacrum. This is several inches below the navel and the same distance into the body's interior. [fig. 1]

In the four-legged animal, body weight is transferred from the spine through the sacrum, then down the back legs in a simple perpendicular line into the ground. [fig. 2] With like support through the front legs, such a creature is extremely stable (a cat, like a table,

fig. 1—Representation of a side view of a human skeleton. In the erect standing position, the spine holds the head, rib cage, and pelvis so that they are bisected by the line of gravity and are therefore centered one directly over the other. The line of weight transfer from the spine through the sacrum, however, falls notably behind the line of gravity.

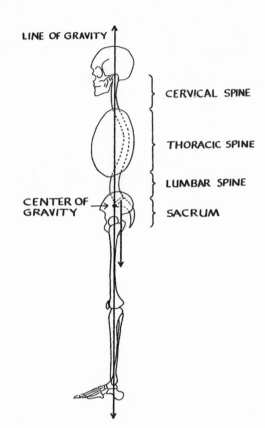

LINE OF GRAVITY

CERVICAL SPINE

THORACIC SPINE

LUMBAR SPINE

CENTER OF GRAVITY

SACRUM

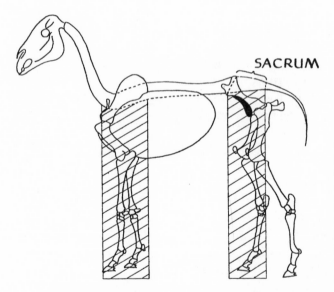

SACRUM

fig. 2—Representation of a side view of a horse skeleton. This varies significantly from the human skeleton in that: a) the spine is parallel rather than perpendicular to the ground; b) the spine is supported at two ends rather than one; c) the sacrum is centered directly over the pelvis and back legs rather than behind them as in the human. These features provide the horse with greater stability, but less flexibility than humans.

is not easily unbalanced). Such a structure, however, does not allow for wielding tools or dancing like Isadora Duncan. Having freed the arms for complex self-expressive movement by standing the spine upright and perpendicular rather than parallel to the ground, human beings must pay the price of having a somewhat less stable pelvis.

The spine must sit on the sacrum behind the point where the pelvis sits on the legs so that weight now transfers through it and forward, as well as down to the legs. Thus the pelvis can still be centered over the legs and yet provide the base for a vertical spine.

Just as humankind used the arch structure to build the apparently delicate upwardly soaring gothic cathedrals, so too the arch appears in nature to provide strong weight support with a minimum of building material. An arch is composed of two columns that fall toward each other. The space between them is filled by a wedge called a keystone that does not allow them to fall together any further. [fig. 3] Since the columns are falling with equal force in opposite directions, they counterbalance each other. Any weight placed on top of the keystone cannot fall down because the keystone is wider on top and cannot fall through the narrower space below. Weight placed over the columns only makes them thrust with greater force toward each other and wedge the keystone more firmly in place. As a result, the greater the weight placed on top of the arch, the more firmly it stands.

The sacrum is in appearance and in fact the keystone of an arch that supports the spine. [fig. 4] The pillars of the arch are formed by the thickened portions of the two os innominata. These pillars have their base at the femoral joints, where the heads of the femurs or thigh bones fit into sockets in the pelvis when standing, or when sitting, at the rocker-shaped parts of the lower end of the pelvis called the tuberosities of the ischia. This arch, called the posterior arch of the pelvis, supports and transfers the downward thrust of the weight of the spine to the legs and ground. The anterior arch of the pelvis counterbalances the forward weight thrust from spine to femoral joints. The keystone for this arch is the cartilage at the mid-front of the pelvis called the pubic symphysis, and the pillars are the two arms of bone on either side that brace against the dual bases of the pillars of the posterior arch.

Further reinforcement of the sides of the pelvis, to counterbalance the outward weight thrust from the sacrum at center body

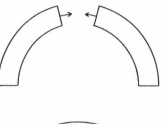
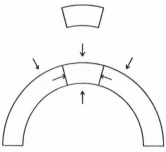

fig. 3—Three arches explained in text: a) two pillars, b) keystone, c) full arch.

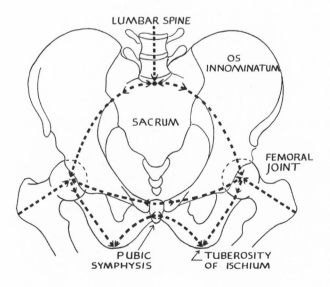

fig. 4—Front view of a human pelvis. The posterior arch, whose keystone is the sacrum and whose pillars are the thickened portions of the os innominata, supports the weight of the spine and transfers it outward, downward and forward to the femoral joints and the tuberosities of the ischia. The anterior arch, whose keystone is the pubic symphysis and whose pillars are the arms of bone radiating from it, thrusts backward to counterbalance the forward thrust of the posterior arch. The femurs thrust upward and inward against the downward and outward thrust of the posterior arch.

sideways to the femoral joints, is provided by the shape of the femurs. These bones are bent to angle inward as well as upward to support the bases of the pillars from the outside inward against any tendency to spread apart. This kind of bracing is called a buttress and was likewise used by medieval architects to support the relatively thin walls of their cathedrals without blocking the flow of light through vast stained glass windows.

The pelvis surpasses a cathedral in complexity, however, because the pillars of the cathedral rest on solid ground but those of the pelvis rest on the spherical tops of two very moveable legs. In this respect, the pelvis shares something of the quality of a seesaw. [fig. 5] On one end (the sacrum) sits the considerable weight of the upper body and spine. Very little weight sits on the other end (the pubic symphysis) of the seesaw while the legs thrust up from the ground underneath to push it further upward. This would seem to create an embarrassing situation in which the front of the pelvic seesaw would fly up and hit us in the chin unless we exerted considerable effort with the muscles that pass from the front of the thigh to the front of the pelvis in order to hold it down onto the legs. This does not happen due to the holding power of the Y or ileofemoral ligament which is a thick, tough, virtually inelastic, band of fiber that holds the front of the pelvis down onto the head of the femur. [fig. 6] Because this ligament is so tight across the

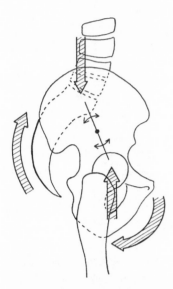

fig. 5—Side view of the pelvis with the spine thrusting down on the back of it and the femurs thrusting up on the front, counterbalanced by the action of the Y-ligament.

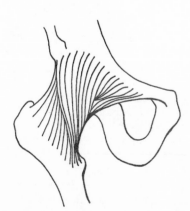

fig. 6—Front view of the one femoral joint covered by the "Y" shaped ileofemoral or Y-ligament.

fig. 7—Side view of a dancer performing an arabesque. The pelvis moves like a seesaw whose fulcrum is the head of the femur of the standing leg. The Y-ligament of the backward-moving leg pulls the front of the pelvis downward along with it, forcing the back of the pelvis and low spine upward and forward in response.

front of the femoral joints, it pulls the front of the pelvis down strongly enough to cause the back of the pelvis to thrust up against the weight of the spine, thus balancing the seesaw. It is easy to see this action of the Y-ligament when we raise our leg behind us as in an arabesque so that the pelvis is forced to tilt further down in front and up in back with the lumbar spine hyperextending to compensate and maintain our chest and head upright. [fig. 7] The slight limitation to our movement range in the hip joints that the Y-ligament imposes is more than made up for by its stabilizing properties that save us from the necessity of a great deal of constant muscle work to maintain erect posture.

So far, I have only mentioned bones and ligament in my discussion of the perfect balances of forces ideally found in the pelvis. Few of us, however, have found this state in which our pelvis balances on top of our legs and under our spine with only minimal muscular exertion. I remember my great distress when I first became aware of my pelvis as something to be aligned in relation to the rest of me. In front of the mirror at age eleven I was shocked to see my pelvis protruding behind me in what seemed to be gargantuan proportions. For the next ten years I tried to rectify the situation, to no avail, by strongly contracting my buttocks, back thigh, and abdominal muscles in hopes of forcing my pelvis unobtrusively under me. [fig. 8] And I also bumped, rolled, and bounced my derriere on the floor at every opportunity, fervently praying, "Wear out!" I did succeed in acquiring overdeveloped, hard buttocks and low back and abdominal muscles. This not only gave more definition to my behind but also made it impossible for me to flex my spine enough to touch the floor with my fingertips when my knees were extended, or to kick my leg higher than shin level. Weeping with frustration after ballet class, I thought, "If I am this stiff at age eleven, what will become of me as a grown-up?"

I also noticed that when I was not actively "holding in my stomach" my pelvis seemed to perversely "compensate" by hiking up in back so that my spine arched uncomfortably backward while my belly visibly preceded me. [fig. 9] In this backwardly arching position, I had to jut my chin forward and up in order to face the world. By the time I reached college I had grown accustomed to headaches, a stiff neck and low back, and buttocks like boulders: hard, large, and always cold to touch.

It was not until I became an official grown-up, twenty-one years old, that I learned from Dr. Sweigard how to effectively "get rid of my derriere" and "loosen up" enough to be able to dance in the process. The first thing I learned was that my back, or anyone else's back, is not flat because the spine is composed of three counterbalancing curves. It was certainly a relief to know that my inability to flatten my spine against a wall while standing with "good posture" was not due to deformity. The spine connects the three main weight centers of the trunk consisting of the head, rib cage and pelvis at the

fig. 8—Side view of a dancer who is "tucking" her pelvis. Muscles in the buttocks and lower thoracic spine area must be held in a strong contraction to maintain an exaggeratedly flattened back. Muscles on the front of the thighs and back of the calves must be held in strong contraction to keep from falling over when the pelvis is thrust slightly forward of the legs.

fig. 9—Side view of a dancer who has "retracted" her pelvis so that the front tilts downward. This tilts the back of the pelvis and lumbar spine to exaggerate the spinal curves. In order to remain upright excessive muscle contraction is required in the low back and in the back of the neck.

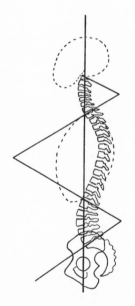

fig. 10—A schematic side view of the spine and pelvis with the head and rib cage locations indicated. The curves of the spine and the tilt of the pelvis all counterbalance each other. If one curve is exaggerated, then the others can likewise increase to maintain upright posture.

back of the body so that there can be independent movement between these three parts. At the same time, the spine curves inward toward center body to support directly underneath the head and rib cage, stabilizing them over the pelvis. In order to efficiently serve this dual purpose of giving flexibility and stability to the trunk, the spine must curve. These curves can counterbalance each other so that if one is more pronounced another can likewise increase its curvature. However relatively flat or round each of our spines appears, we all have the potential to align our head, rib cage and pelvis so that they balance one precisely over the other. [fig. 10]

Distorting one of the spinal curves, as I did when I arched my back or tucked my pelvis under me, throws these three weights out of line with each other. This in turn requires extra muscle work to keep the unbalanced structure from toppling over. Remember how your tower of building blocks in nursery school collapsed in a heap when you did not center the blocks directly over each other? This same principle applies to our body. In order to maintain our pelvis out of line with the rest of our trunk, we must apply extra force to keep ourselves upright. This force is muscle action. Muscles that are continuously contracted become hypertonic. This means that they are not only very large, hard and strong but they are also able to stretch very little and therefore limit the movement range severely at the joints that they cross over. Such muscle "strength" is clearly disaster for dancers who want to have the fullest possible mobility at all their joints. This property of constantly worked muscles explains why the harder I worked to hide my derriere, the larger, firmer, and less flexible I became in that area.

Dr. Sweigard showed me that I had to concern myself with balancing my bones so that I wouldn't need to work so hard to stand erect or move. This idea was totally revolutionary for me and yet it is simple, obvious, and works.

Since the spine connects the pelvis to the upper body in back we do not need to hold the back of our pelvis up in defiance of gravity. Any effort to do so only gives us hypertonic low back muscles and a prominent derriere. Since the pelvis has weight just like any other substance, we do not need to hold it down in back either by contracting our buttocks or back thigh muscles. Simply imagining the sacrum as being very heavy so that it drops down toward the ground behind the heels allows the pelvis to fall into place underneath us without effort. This also lengthens the spine without destroying the curves that belong in it.

It is important to watch the sacrum drop down as if on a plumb line in your mind's eye only. Any active effort on your part will increase your muscles' work and defeat the whole purpose of centering the pelvis in the first place. You may find it easier to accomplish centering your body by thinking about what you're doing rather than just doing it; stand with your eyes closed, arms hanging and your feet pointing straight ahead supporting you directly in line with your femoral and knee joints. Your femoral joint is located deep in the center of your leg just inside the tendon that pops up at the "crease" between your thigh and pelvis when you flex there. [fig. 11] Now you can actually let your knees bend under the weight of your sacrum dropping in space, as well as in your imagination, towards the ground behind your heels. Make sure that your pelvis goes straight down a perpendicular in relation to the floor, not forward or back of you. Deviation from your "plumb line" requires your low back, buttocks, or abdominal muscles to contract. In fact they should soften and release. [fig. 12]

Once you find your pelvis falling under your rib cage like a bell clapper from a bell at rest, you can rise back up to your full height on your legs, thinking all the while of your sacrum continuing to

fig. 11—Front view of flexion of the thigh on the pelvis at the femoral joint. The joint is located at the center of the top of the thigh just inside the place where a muscle tendon bulges out when you flex at your hip joint.

fig. 12—Side view of someone imagining that the sacrum is so heavy that it actually sinks down toward the ground behind the heels, and that the central axis is rising upward so that the top of the head moves skyward.

sink downward. Locking your knees into a hyperextended position when you arise will tilt your pelvis up in back, so bring your knees to a full extension in line with your femoral and ankle joints, not behind them. Repeat this action of moving down and up your central axis very slowly. Give yourself enough time to make sure you avoid any unnecessary muscular effort or deviation of your pelvis. Even slightly pulling your pelvis under you is still "tucking" and can result in some muscles working overtime, becoming hypertonic, while their opposers become lazy or hypotonic. A balance of muscle action around your joints is only possible if your weight is transferred through the centers of your joints and mostly through bone instead of soft tissues. In tucking, your pelvis is thrust forward so that its weight is transferred through the front of the legs, and the thigh muscles have to work to stabilize it, while the muscles of the calves remain contracted in order to keep you from falling forward. More destructive than the loss of flexibility of spine and femoral joints due to the continuously contracting muscles around these parts is the pressure on the nerves existing and entering the spinal cord through a lumbar spine distorted by forceful flattening.

In attempting to "hold your stomach in" you may be actually "tucking." If your pelvis is hanging directly under your head and rib cage it will be supporting your abdominal contents from underneath so that they will not spill out the front if you "let go." Your weight can now continue to sink down to transfer through the whole of each foot, not just through toes or heels. Enjoy this sense of being totally grounded through your feet as they stand directly under you.

If you turn your legs out for dance, you need make no adjustments in your pelvis. This is a femoral joint movement, not a pelvic one. The muscles that rotate your legs outward at the femoral joints are deep underneath your gluteal muscles, the big buttock muscles you can see and feel, so that your buttocks should stay soft when you turn out your legs. [fig. 13] As a result you will be able to kick your leg high to the front without taking your pelvis along too, because you do not have to fight your buttock muscles to do so.

Some of us, after long experience with losing our balance, keep up a mistrustful battle with gravity. It is not easy for us to give up holding our bodies away from the ground as we stand. If you still find stubbornly hard muscles in your body, communicate a more precise purpose to them. If your buttock (gluteus maximus) is overexerting, think of your sacrum moving downward. It is as if your sacrum were expanding, opening, or radiating downward and outward from center. By imagining this you are actually allowing the floor to support you rather than you holding up the floor with unnecessarily contracted muscles. [fig. 14]

When you release this excess holding, the heads of the femurs can sink more easily and deeply into their sockets in the pelvis, closer toward the center of gravity. The centering process makes it much easier to control large range leg movement from the femoral joints with a minimum of work. [fig. 15] Thus I can experience what a great dance teacher once said to me, "You must be like a grape whose hard seed is at the center while the sweet juices flow softly around it."

Check to make sure you are only thinking and not actually doing any of the imagined activities. Notice if you are holding your breath, or breathing irregularly or forcefully. If your lower back muscles (erector spinae) are tense and bulging backward, imagine your lumbar vertebrae moving forward toward the direction you are facing. Be especially careful to only imagine this and not perform or do it. The goal is to re-establish your natural lumbar curve, not distort it. [fig. 16] Since our thinking directs our movement, this mental picture will actually cause the deep muscles that pass from the front of the femurs to the lumbar spine's front surface to come into action. They are deep underneath your superficial abdominal muscles and so you cannot feel them work. If you do get a sensation of contraction along the front of your pelvis and spine, then you are doing, not thinking, and are defeating yourself. A basic principle of muscle action called reciprocal innervation ensures that when a muscle contracts on one side of a joint the muscle on the opposite side of the joint will release to an equal degree. This principle is operating to your advantage when you only imagine the connection from your femoral joints to your lumbar spine. As the deep psoas muscles begin to act on the front of your lumbar spine, the big erector spinae muscles on either side of your low back will release to an equal degree. An indicator that you are imagining correctly, and only imagining, is that your

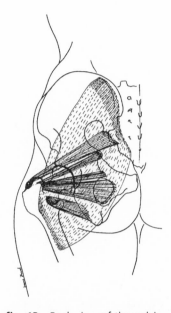

fig. 13—Back view of the pelvis showing the gluteus maximus muscle with dotted lines, and the underlying six deep outward rotator muscles with unbroken lines.

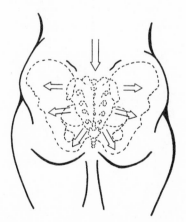

fig. 14—Drawing of the back of the pelvis. The imagined action being illustrated is watching the sacrum moving and expanding downward and outward to the sides.

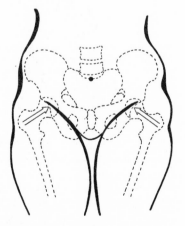

fig. 15—Drawing of the front of the pelvis. The imagined action being illustrated is watching the heads of the femurs sinking more deeply into their sockets.

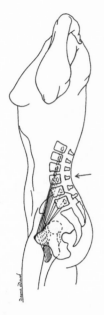

fig. 16—Drawing of the far side of the lumbar spine, pelvis, and thigh. The imagined action being illustrated is watching the lumbar vertebrae moving forward so that a small arch is formed in the lower back. Represented is the line of action of the psoas muscle that goes from the inner top of the thigh bone (lesser trochanter of the femur) to each vertebra of the lumbar spine and the last vertebra of the thoracic spine (T12). The psoas can pull each of these six vertebral bodies forward so as to increase the lumbar curve.

lumbar spine will feel slightly indented or concave to your touch; yet the erector spinae muscles on either side of it will be softer and more pliant than before.

Now, for aesthetic reasons, you may want to gather your abdominal contents inward slightly, by drawing your belly toward the front of your lumbar spine. Imagine that your belly button (umbilicus) and the middle of your lower back (third lumbar vertebra) are magnetically attracted to each other.

I like to visualize my abdominal organs as a "visceral ball" that is contained between my abdominal wall muscles in front (external abdominal oblique, internal abdominal oblique, transversus abdominus, and rectus abdominus) and my psoas muscle in back. The abdominal wall muscles can contract to narrow the ball, draw it backward toward the front of the spine, and roll it upward toward the rib cage. The psoas muscle can contract to send the ball forward and roll it downward towards the pelvis. If one overly activates the abdominal wall muscles or underengages the psoas muscles, the ball rolls so far back that one's lumbar spine flattens or reverses its curve to bulge to the back. This creates difficulties for the intervertebral discs of the spine and the back muscles. If one overly activates the psoas muscles or underengages the abdominal wall muscles, the ball rolls so far forward that one's belly pokes out in front. This creates difficulties for a person's self-image and the abdominal organs which

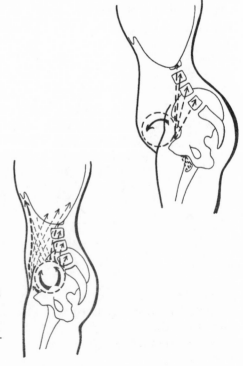

fig. 17—Schematic rendition of the "visceral ball" contained within the pelvis from a side view. On the left, the abdominal wall moves the ball towards midline, upward, and backward. On the right, the psoas moves the ball downward and forward. In the center, the abdominal wall and the psoas function together to maintain the ball in equilibrium.

are now bulging outward and downward. However, if both the abdominal wall and psoas muscles are working equally, the "visceral ball" is gently "embraced" on all sides, maintaining an attractive and comfortable equilibrium within the bony ring of the pelvis. [fig. 17]

Stand quietly with eyes closed for a moment and be aware of how your body feels now without making any postural adjustments or self-judgments. Sometimes we feel out of balance when we alter some of our habitual patterns of muscle activity, but our sensations can be deceptive. Ask a friend or look in a mirror to see if you are actually more or less centered than before.

You are now centering your pelvis in relation to the rest of your body, but it is not in a position. It is an ever-dynamic balance that allows you your fullest possible range of movement with the least possible muscle work.

Standing on Two Legs,
or Even One

The first creature to stand on two legs is long extinct. Dinosaurs running on two legs swiftly overtook their four-legged prey. These dinosaurs remained erect by means of the stabilizing effect of a long tail, widespread feet with huge toes, and flexed knees giving them a broader base of support and lowering their center of gravity. Such stability resulted in the pelvis having no skeletal support directly under it, and thus gargantuan bones with enormously strong and bulky leg muscles were required to sustain upright balance.[fig. 1]

In contrast, the human skeleton is structured so that all the joints of the leg from the pelvis to the feet can be directly in the line of gravity, perpendicular to the ground. This gives us the potential for having a streamlined leg with less bulgy and very flexible muscles since they have to do a minimum of work to hold our bones up against the pull of gravity. Deviation from this ideal alignment of joints creates excess muscle tension, loss of movement range, and increased probability of being injured during strenuous activity. With this in mind, let us examine the construction of our lower extremities more carefully.

Our pelvis rests on the two round tops of the femurs (thigh bones). Ideally the pelvis is balanced evenly from front to back on these femoral heads. These joints between the pelvis and the femurs are called the femoral joints (often referred to as the hip joints). Because they are ball and socket joints, it is possible for us to move our legs quite freely in all directions in relation to a stable pelvis

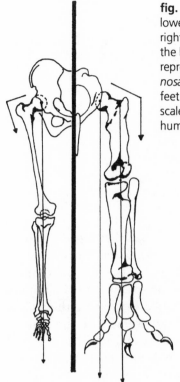

fig. 1—Front view: A dinosaur lower extremity is shown on the right, human lower extremity on the left. The dinosaur skeleton represented comes from *Tyrannosaurus Rex,* approximately 20 feet tall and 50 feet long, and is scaled down to match the human skeleton.

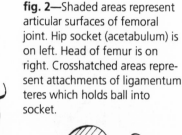

fig. 2—Shaded areas represent articular surfaces of femoral joint. Hip socket (acetabulum) is on left. Head of femur is on right. Crosshatched areas represent attachments of ligamentum teres which holds ball into socket.

(movement of the leg to the back is somewhat limited due to the shortness of a strong ligament called the ileofemoral ligament which crosses the front of the joint). [fig. 2, 3] The part of the femur just below the head, called the neck of the femur, angles out to the side of the pelvis, allowing us to flex more freely at the joint without having the front of the femur collide with the front of the pelvis. The long part of the femur, called the shaft of the femur, angles back inward so that it ends to meet the lower leg bone, the tibia, directly in line with the femoral joint. The knee joint falls in the line of gravity of the femoral joint only in humans. In other vertebrates the shaft of the femur goes straight down, perpendicular to the ground from the base of the femoral neck (greater trochanter), and therefore in a line outside the line of gravity of the femoral joint. [fig. 1]

The femoral joint is very unlikely to dislocate due to the great depth of the socket and the large and powerful ligaments that hold the head of the femur in place. In contrast, the knee consists essentially of the femur resting precariously on the extremely shallow indentation of the top of the tibia. Some reinforcement is provided by a series of delicate ligaments which cross inside of the joint called the anterior and posterior cruciate ligaments. [fig. 4] Because of the way in which they attach, they cause a slight rotation within the knee itself when the knee goes from full extension to slight flexion, and

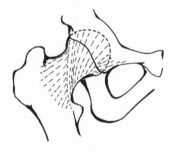

fig. 3—Front view of right femoral joint. Dotted lines covering front surface of joint represent the ileofemoral or Y-ligament.

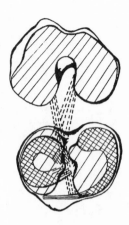

fig. 4—Articular surfaces of right knee joint. Inside of knee is on right, outside is on left. Crosshatching represents semilunar cartilages or menisci. Dotted lines represent anterior and posterior cruciate ligaments connecting tibia to femur above.

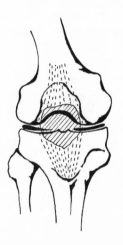

fig. 5—Front view of right knee joint. Tibia supports femur. Fibula buttresses tibia on outside of lower leg (left side of picture). Dark wedges between bones represent menisci, shaded area patella. Dotted lines represent tendon of quadriceps femoris muscle which encapsulates patella and connects to tuberosity of tibia below.

vice versa. There are also two pieces of cartilage that move independently between the femur and the tibia called the menisci or semilunar cartilages. Because these are only loosely attached to the ligament that surrounds the knee joint, they are easily torn if the joint sustains an extreme twisting movement while supporting the weight of the body. If the knee is habitually held out of line with the femoral and ankle joints, continuous imbalanced muscle work is required from the muscles of the thigh and the calf to protect it. This will result in overdeveloped and habitually sore or painful legs as well as an increasingly unstable knee.

Although our kneecap (called the patella) is the bony landmark which obviously locates our knee, it is not part of the joint proper. The knee cap actually floats over the front of the joint, encased in the tendon of the quadriceps femoris muscles, the ones that form the front of the thigh. When these muscles are contracted, they lift and tighten the kneecap. [fig. 5] The kneecap serves as a protection to the front of the joint and also increases the efficiency of the quadriceps muscles.

The knee is a hinge joint which primarily flexes and extends. Rotation between the femur and tibia is possible only when the knee is flexed (or when it is hyperextended so that the knee is locked into a position in which it "faces" inward while the ankle and foot "face" straight ahead). Rotation is freest when the femur and the tibia are at a ninety degree angle in relation to each other. As the knee is extended, any rotation is reversed to bring the fronts of the ankle, knee, and femoral joints back to "face" all in the same direction again.

The ankle is also a hinge joint but a more stable one than the knee. No rotation is possible here. There is only flexion and extension at this joint (other movement takes place between the twenty-six bones of the foot itself). Beside having exceedingly strong ligamentous support across both the inside and the outside of the joint, the ankle also has bony reinforcement on either side of it. The tibia forms a sort of roof and inside wall while the fibula (the outside lower leg bone

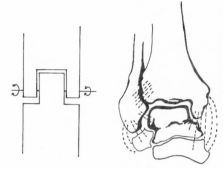

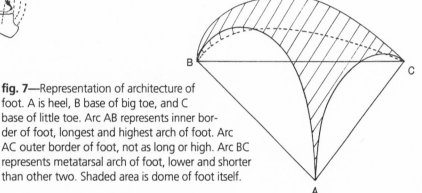

fig. 6—Front view of right ankle. Dotted lines represent ligaments that connect tibia to inside of foot (far right), fibula to outside of foot (left), tibia to fibula (center). Drawing at left represents hinge action of ankle joint.

fig. 7—Representation of architecture of foot. A is heel, B base of big toe, and C base of little toe. Arc AB represents inner border of foot, longest and highest arch of foot. Arc AC outer border of foot, not as long or high. Arc BC represents metatarsal arch of foot, lower and shorter than other two. Shaded area is dome of foot itself.

that buttresses the tibia) forms an outside wall. Together these bones, joined by a flexible yet strong ligament, house the talus (bone of the top of the foot) encasing it on three sides.[fig. 6]

The foot itself is composed of lengthwise and crosswise arches so that each foot is somewhat like a dome with a triangular base.[fig. 7] Ideally, when we are standing still, the weight of the leg transfers from the ankle equally forward and back, one half of the weight going through the heel and one half going through the ball of the foot. With the feet pointing straight ahead so that the center of the knee is in line with the base of the third toe, the weight of the entire body is being supported by the fundamental arches of the feet.[fig. 8] This longitudinal arch, reinforced by ligaments, can hold us up without the aid of any muscle work at all within the foot itself. When we are moving through space, this arch functions as a powerful spring to thrust us forward from one foot to the other through the action of a multitude of muscles on the sole of the foot and back of the leg. When we put the foot back down again, all these muscles relax as long as our foot is pointing straight ahead so that our weight is again supported by the fundamental arch. This regular alternation between relaxation and contraction of the foot and leg muscles gives us the capacity to walk for a very long time without fatigue (and in the process greatly aids blood circulation through our legs). If the foot is maintained in a turned-out position, with the toes raised, or curled continuously, muscles through the entire leg and foot are being contracted constantly in standing and walking. This causes the legs to become rapidly fatigued and sore with even a little exertion.

Poor alignment of the pelvis and spine and locking or hyperexten-

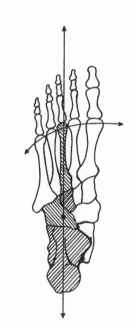

fig. 8—Sole of right foot (plantar surface). Shaded area indicates bones that form fundamental arch of foot: calcaneus (heel bone), cuboid bone (marked with a black dot to indicate that it is keystone of fundamental arch), third cuneiform bone, and third metatarsal bone.

sion of the knees are just a couple of the other factors that can throw the joints of the leg out of line with each other, creating excessive fatigue, pain, or limitation in the movement range of the legs.

Whatever the cause that might hold your legs askew, the aim to keep in mind is allowing the joints to come easily into line with one another. This is possible only if your feet are pointing straight ahead (lines drawn from centers of heels to centers of base of third toe should be exactly parallel) and are standing directly under your femoral joints (located at the center of the "crease" where your leg meets your pelvis). You might rock your pelvis forward and back lightly like a swing moving in a slight breeze until you feel that your weight is evenly supported by the entire feet: half the weight through the heels, half through the balls of the feet. Think of your sacrum (the center back of your pelvis that is also the lower end of your spine) as very heavily sinking down toward your heels but do not contract your buttock or abdominal muscles to do this; let gravity do all the work while you simply observe in your mind's eye.

Now turn your attention to one leg at a time. Imagine a line of energy thrusting up from the ground through the center of your foot (the cuboid bone that forms the keystone of the fundamental arch, located just in front of the center of the heel in the part of the foot that doesn't touch the ground) straight up to the center of your femoral joint. Visualize that side of your pelvis being supported by the

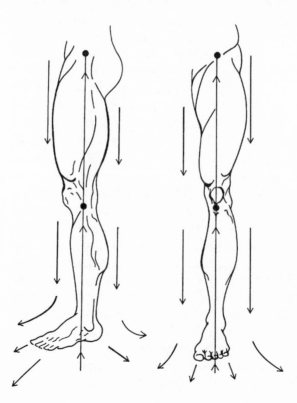

fig. 9—Side and front views of left leg. Arrows show lines of visualized movement.

line of energy rising up to the head of the femur. Think of the centers of your foot, ankle, knee and femoral joint as open gateways for the energy to shoot through from the ground source. This line of energy jets up like a fountain of water from the ground to your pelvis to support you upright and then it streams down from your buttock and all around you like a waterfall to flow out your heels and out each toe in a spreading pool.[fig. 9] Think of bones through the center of the leg as strong and thrusting, and muscles and flesh around the periphery as melting down. If your knee has been locked back into a hyperextended position, you will have to allow it to soften (it may even feel sort of baggy or bent) so that it can come into place directly in line with the centers of the ankle and femoral joints. If your knee was slightly bent, then both your knee joint proper, and your kneecap will rise up on the column of energy to come into line. In either case, as your legs become straighter, the bones will support you and the muscles around your leg can function more easily and adaptively.

Because our legs must support the weight of our entire body much of the day, even a slight deviation from center can result in noticeably uneven muscle development in our legs. It takes time and much movement practice with a new alignment pattern to change this muscle development. Balanced muscle action around the joints becomes a habit only after overused muscles release their excess tension and underused muscles become activated, automatically. In the meantime you must actively concentrate on performing everyday basic movement patterns with your joints in line. Because it is very easy to fall comfortably back into old habit patterns even when you are paying attention, you should use a mirror and the eyes of a good and patient friend to check yourself as you do the following movement practice.

Face a barre or doorway. Hold onto the barre or the sides of the doorway firmly with both hands. Stand with your weight equally distributed over both feet. Bring one foot slightly off the floor by flexing at the femoral joint so that all of your weight is transferred through one leg. Make sure that your pelvis does *not* shift at all as you change from standing on two feet to one. This means that you will have to hold on firmly with your hands to keep your pelvis from moving (as it would have to move slightly if you were standing free). Your standing leg should be easily extended but not locked at the knee. Now shift to both legs again. If you did not move your pelvis in the first place, you will feel no change in its position now. Flex at the other femoral joint in the same way. Return to standing on both legs. Repeat this alternating pattern a number of times slowly enough to be certain that your pelvis is not moving in space at all as you do so. Avoid contracting the muscles around your pelvis such as the buttock or abdominal muscles. You will experience supporting your weight entirely and precisely through the central axis of one leg, both legs, and then the other leg.[fig. 10]

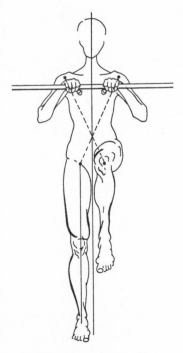

fig. 10—Front view of person flexing at femoral joint without shifting weight. Pelvis remains centered over line of gravity.

Continue the alternating pattern standing free of the barre or doorway. When you raise one leg off the floor, you may raise the opposite arm for counterbalance. Your pelvis will move slightly as you shift from leg to leg, making a figure-eight pattern in space. Keep breathing. Now start moving through space, walking. Visualize your pelvis moving in a serpentine pattern as you shift from foot to foot while moving toward your destination. Walk at varying speeds. Let your arms swing in harmony with your legs. Many of us have the impulse to take our chins or chests ahead of us when we are in a hurry, but we still won't get there any faster than our legs can carry us. Change to walking extremely slowly: like a plant growing, almost imperceptibly. Let your eyes caress every object they touch. Let your feet remember that they are always a living connection with the earth. Step softly, and allow each leg its full capacity to be alternately stable as a column and fluid as water.

In Honor of the Foot

Our feet are what connect us to the ground most of the time. Because the surface of the earth is as constantly variable as ourselves, our feet need to be able to adapt their shape to interface. They are able to do this because each foot is composed of twenty-six bones with at least thirty-three joints between them, allowing movement in all directions. However, the feet do more than just accommodate the surface between ourselves and the earth. They also have an important role in propelling us through space from contact point to contact point. For this, they can become rigid bony levers that thrust the ground away. Thus, our feet have a dual "personality": they are pliant, adaptive, mobile, and receptive to other forces, yet hard, propulsive, stable, and aggressively able to thrust other forms away.

The structure of the foot itself makes its double function possible. Imagine that you have a piece of chain, composed of seven or eight links. Lie it flat down on the ground. You can easily wiggle it so that the links are pushed from side to side with the slightest touch. When the foot is standing flat on the ground, it is similarly responsive. Now imagine that you hold down one end of the chain and twist the other end until the links lock into each other, forming a rigid bar. When the ball of the foot is pushing off the ground, the foot is likewise a stiff lever that thrusts the body away from the ground behind it.

Overall, the foot is shaped like an irregular rectangle, or trape-

37

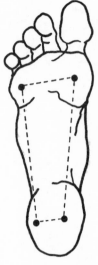

zoid. The front corners of the rectangle are composed of the ball of the big toe and the ball of the little toe, respectively (the toes themselves are a fringe on the end of the rectangle which can aid in stability when necessary). The back corners of the rectangle are composed of the inner border and outer border of the heel, respectively.[fig. 1] Because of the large fat pad protecting the sole of the foot, you cannot see that the heel bone itself (calcaneus) is much higher on the inside than on the outside. In other words, the rectangle has already been twisted from the back.[fig. 2] Between the heel bone and the ball of the foot, there are a number of intermediate joints which lock into place or move freely depending on the degree of twist in the foot.[fig. 3]

Greater mobility/adaptability is required when we are standing on our foot; therefore, the foot untwists so that the medial border of the heel drops somewhat. This action of untwisting is called pronation. If the foot can pronate excessively, we describe it as being "flat" or as having a "fallen arch." Such a foot is so mobile and adaptable that it doesn't support weight well without the work of extra muscles. The stability between the bones of the foot that is required when we push off the ground as in striding, running, and jumping is provided by an increased twisting of the foot called supination. If the foot twists so that the medial border of the heel rises excessively, we describe it as

fig. 1—View looking up at the sole of the right foot. The foot appears as a trapezoid whose front corners are formed by the ball of the big toe and ball of the little toe, and whose back corners are formed by the inside and the outside of the heel bone (calcaneus).

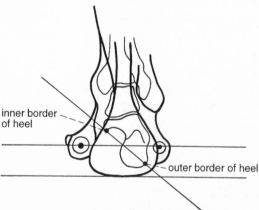

fig. 2—View looking at the back of the right foot. The inside of the heel bone is much higher than the outside of the heel bone, although the large fat pad protecting the sole of the foot conceals this fact. The thicker lines represent an outline of the foot as we see it. Note that the ball of the foot is parallel with the floor while the heel bone is in an oblique relationship, thus producing a twist in the foot's structure.

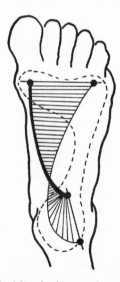

fig. 3—View looking at the top of the right foot which schematically represents the foot as a twisted plate. The dotted line represents the footprint, while the small circles represent the four corners of the trapezoid which appears twisted once the vertical dimension of the foot is included.

being "high-arched" or as an "equinus (horse)" foot. Such a foot is so stable that it doesn't absorb shock well, therefore making its owner prey to shin splints, fractures, and poor adaptation to uneven ground.

Observe the normal shift from a less to a more twisted position of the foot by looking at the height of the inner (medial) ankle bone when you are standing, and then when the weight comes off the foot as you step forward to stand on the other foot. As the weight comes off your foot, its inner ankle bone will become higher. You can see the change in height reversed as you go from just barely touching your foot to the floor as you stride forward, to having your whole foot on the floor with weight on it. Your inner ankle bone will drop lower as your weight goes onto your foot.

Ideally, however much the foot is twisting and untwisting at the heel, there should be enough movement potential in the foot to allow both the ball of the big and little toes to remain in contact with the ground in standing. If you cannot maintain contact with the floor through the ball of the little toe, then you are untwisting too much (pronating). Incidentally, this is very common among dancers who have worked hard to deepen their plié and increase their turnout. If you cannot maintain contact with the floor through the ball of the big toe, then you are overtwisting (supinating). This sort of standing is what I call "the Victorian furniture effect."

In order to ensure the full range of motion between the heel and the entire ball of your foot, practice the following:

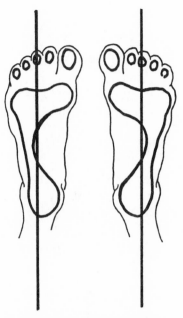

fig. 4—View looking down at the feet flat on the floor. Align the center of your heel and your third toe along the crack between the floorboards. When the feet are anatomically parallel, there is a wedge-shaped space between them.

1) Sit on a chair with your knees bent and your feet flat on the floor in front of you. Plant your feet in a parallel position in line with your hip joints. In order to assume this position, it is helpful to use the cracks between floor boards as a guide. Put the center of your heel and your third toe right on the line. When both feet are arranged in this way, there will be a wedge-shaped space between your feet which is wider at the back and narrower at the front.[fig. 4] Keeping your whole foot planted—both the big and the little toes resting on the floor—slowly open your knees as far as they will go. Then slowly bring them together. Alternate between taking your knees apart and together as far as possible without letting any part of the ball of your foot come off the floor.

2) Remain seated on a chair, or stand up if you want more challenge. Bring one heel off the floor so that you have your weight on the ball of that foot (and the whole surface of the other foot). Now make little circles with the elevated heel while keeping the entire ball of the foot fixed firmly on the floor. After making a few circles, start making parabolas (describing the motion of a swing through space) with that heel. Make the parabolas as large as possible without losing contact of any part of the ball of the foot with the floor. Repeat on the other foot.[fig. 5]

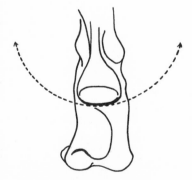

fig. 5—View looking at the back of the right foot. Describe a parabolic curve with your heel in space while keeping the ball of your foot completely in contact with the floor.

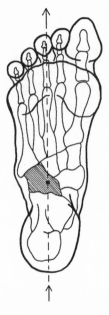

fig. 6—View looking up at the sole of the right foot. When we walk correctly, it appears that the center of the knee travels directly above the pathway shown by the arrow from center of heel through the third toe. The shaded bone is the cuboid bone, keystone of the foot.

These two practices not only increase the joint motion in your foot and gently strengthen the muscles that control that motion, but they also prepare you for the actions your foot will appropriately perform when you walk.

When we walk correctly, it appears that the center of our heel strikes the floor; then we track through our foot right through its central axis which passes from the center of the heel through the third toe, and finally come off the ball of our foot with our knee directly over our third toe. If your gait has this appearance, then you probably have excellent mechanical use of your legs, and happy knees.[fig. 6]

However, this appearance of a straightforward alignment of all the joints of your leg conceals a very complex choreography of the foot which is taking place simultaneously. Ideally, when your heel strikes the floor, it strikes more toward the outside of the foot (and through the vertical axis of the heel bone itself). Then, as you put weight on your foot to come into the standing position, your weight will roll toward the inside of the foot. This rolling inward serves to absorb the shock of landing on the ground and also serves to make the foot more adaptable to the ground (that is, the foot is untwisting in the process). Next, as your heel comes off the floor and the weight goes to the ball of your foot, you will roll again toward the outside of the foot, and onto the outside of the ball of the foot. This rolling outward serves to bring the foot back into a more twisted position so that it can lever your weight off the ground and forward into space. Finally, the foot returns to a less twisted position once it no longer has any weight in it and it is pushing off the toes. The last toe to push off is the big toe, as it is the thickest, and usually the longest, of the toes, thus more able to give the last bit of thrust away from the ground. By performing this serpentine dance, the foot is able to fulfill its roles of both shock absorption and thrust exquisitely.[fig. 7]

In some ways, the most difficult thing that the foot has to do is to stand. This is especially true when you are standing balanced on one foot only. In this circumstance, the foot has to be somewhat mobile because the rest of your body does not stay perfectly still relative to the ground, and yet the foot has to be very stable in order to support you. You will remember that the foot is in its more mobile mode when we are standing on it; therefore, the challenge in standing is to keep stable. In order to insure mobile stability, it is useful to recall the image of the foot as a tripod-based dome (always a stable structure). The three supporting points are the ball of the big toe, the ball of the little toe, and the center of the heel bone. The dome is the rest of the foot with a keystone (cuboid bone) at the point of the foot just in front of the part of the heel that leaves a footprint.[fig. 8] If you are looking down at the top of the foot, the keystone is just in front of the center of the ankle joint where the lower leg meets the top of

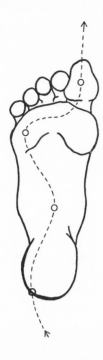

fig. 7—View looking up at the sole of the right foot. The dotted line illustrates how we track our weight through the foot ideally. The small circles indicate the moment of heel strike, mid-stance, heel off, and toe off.

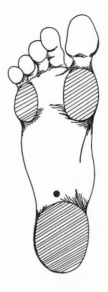

fig. 8—Sole of right foot. Shaded areas show parts that normally make fullest contact with floor. Solid circle indicates the keystone of the foot.

the foot. Imagine that the weight of your body being supported by the foot is equally divided between the three points. If there is not enough weight in your heel, rock your pelvis backward in space slightly so that your sitting bones (ischial tuberosities) are poised behind your heels. If there is not enough weight in the ball of your foot, rock your pelvis slightly forward.

If there is not enough weight on the outside of your foot, in the ball of the little toe, you can do one of several things. You can imagine that you have a tornado starting at your sitting bone, or greater trochanter, that is spiraling outward as it moves toward the center of your heel. You can imagine that you have a waterfall pouring down the outside of your leg, starting from the outside of your hip, passing down along the outside of your knee, down the outside of your ankle and finally forming a pool of water under the outside of your foot. You can also watch that waterfall send rivulets through your little toe, making it grow longer. Taking a more direct approach, you might turn out your thighs slightly so that your knees point out over your third toes.

If there is not enough weight on the inside of your foot, on the ball of the big toe, you also have several options. You can think of your big toe growing long out along the floor. You can visualize all three points moving apart—the toes forward and apart and the heel backward away from them. As you imagine the three points moving apart, think of a space (or an eye) opening up between them, a receptive aperture through which energy can come in from the earth.

Sometimes it really helps to massage the soles of your feet in order to get them to spread on the floor, thus providing a broader base of support. In addition, "neutralizing" the involuntary activity of your muscles first makes it easier to use those muscles more appropriately when you need them for support. A technique for getting deep specific pressure is to press with your thumb into the desired point, then move the bones and joints that lie under that point by manipulating the bones/joint with the other hand. Start with your ankle. Put your thumb just below the inner ankle bone (medial malleolus). Use your other hand to grasp your foot and move it so as to produce circles of your foot on your leg. Sustain the pressure with your thumb for several circles, then move your thumb over a bit closer to the front of the ankle and repeat the procedure. Keep on doing this until you have inched your thumb all the way across the front of the ankle (as if you were tracing an anklet) to end just below your outer ankle bone (lateral malleolus). Now slide your thumb down along the inner border of the foot (the part that touches the other foot when you bring your feet together). Start directly below the inner ankle bone and inch your thumb along until you reach the ball of the big toe. Repeat the same action on the outer border of the foot, moving from below the outer ankle bone to the ball of the little toe. Now work along the sole of the foot. Slide your thumb along the bones (tarsal/metatarsal bones) that go from the bottom of your heel to your big toe. Then slide along the space between the big toe and the second toe (interosseus membrane). Next slide along the bones going to the second toe, etc. Go along the line of each toe and then between the toes. Gently wiggle the bones that go from the heel to the big toe against the bones that go from the heel to the second toe, etc. Also gently circle each toe on its base making sure that you pull on it only very very lightly. Finally, spread the bones of the feet sideways with the same action you would use to fan a deck of cards between your two hands.

After massaging one foot only, stand up and walk around. Stand on that foot and then on the other foot. Do they feel any different? How is your balance? How does it feel to walk on each foot? What does the rest of your leg feel like? How hard does the floor feel to each foot? Are the balls of your big toe and little toe sharing equal weight?

Paradoxically, by relaxing your foot, you may have made it more stable. Nonetheless, finely controlled action in the relevant muscles is needed to maintain that stability when other parts of your body are moving or when the floor under you (as in the subway or a boat) is moving. Since our bodies are never entirely still, such muscle activity is necessary all the time although it may be so brief and slight as to never come to our conscious awareness.

You can test strength and agility in the muscles that cross your ankle joint by doing foot circles against resistance (have a friend hold your foot and try to move it in the opposite direction from the one you are circling it in). Stand up on one leg (hold onto something for balance) and alternately rise onto the ball of your foot so that you are raising your heel off the floor (dancer's relevé), and then rock to your heel raising the toes and ball of the foot off the floor. Put your other foot on top of the ball of the foot you are standing on to provide some resistance to the raising of the front of your foot. You should be able to do this easily twenty to thirty times in quick succession keeping your knee straight. Now try to do it in the same way but keeping your knee flexed. In addition, stand with both feet flat on the floor and alternately raise the outer then the inner borders of the feet off the floor (your inner ankle bones will be moving together and then apart) twenty to thirty times. Next stand on the ball of one foot and alternately roll your ankle inward and then outward twenty to thirty times (hold onto something for balance), repeat on the other side.

After your exertions, stand with the balls of your feet on a door sill or a book and drop your heels to the floor for thirty seconds with your knees straight and then bent. This will lengthen your calves.

If you find that you cannot perform these actions easily, they might be a good series to work on to improve your balance and ankle control. Start with just a few (perhaps four or five) repetitions of each one daily and gradually add one more repetition every two days.

Because our feet are usually bound in shoes, few of us have much control over the small muscles that lie within the foot itself (intrinsic muscles of the foot). Despite strong ankles, we don't make the powerful and elegant usage of our feet that we are ultimately capable of. Without control of these intrinsic muscles, we lack the ability to successfully point our foot or push off in a jump. The following series of movement practices will exercise and educate these intrinsic muscles of your feet.

1) With the sole of your foot on the floor, put your finger on the outside of the big toe. Now try to push the finger away with your toe so that the toe moves outward along the floor away from the other toes. If you have difficulty, try stroking along the inner border of your foot moving in the direction from big toe to heel. You might also massage in the space between the ball of the big toe and the second toe. Keep trying to fan your big toe away from the other toes at least ten times, even if you see no motion. Place your finger on the inner border of the foot and note if you feel any activity in this region, as this is where the muscle that performs the movement is located.

2) Now repeat the same action with the little toe. Put your finger on the outside of your little toe and push it away with the toe so that the toe moves along the floor away from the other toes. You can stroke along the outer border of the foot from toe to heel, to stimulate the muscle which is producing the movement.

3) Fan both the big toe and the little toe away from each other at the same time so that you are performing both 1) and 2).

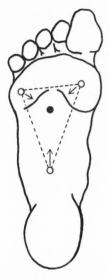

fig. 9—View looking up at the sole of the right foot. The open circles represent the three points that must draw together in order to perform "doming." Place your finger on the filled-circle location of your own foot and then try to grasp or "suction up" that finger with your foot.

4) Draw an imaginary triangle on the sole of your foot that connects the points at the ball of the big toe, the ball of the little toe, and the point in the center of the sole of the foot just in front of the heel (the part that never gets dirty). Put your finger in the middle of this triangle. Try to grasp your finger with the sole of your foot. I call this action "doming" because the top front portion of the foot should actually dome up when you perform it. Make sure that you are not gripping, curling, or thrusting with your toes. Your toes should be completely relaxed. The muscles working are on the sole of your foot, right along the line demarking the triangle. These muscles are important in protecting the metatarsal arch. [fig. 9]

5) Fan both the big and little toes while simultaneously doming the foot. You may find this easier to do with your foot resting lightly on the floor, without weight on it (so do this sitting down).

6) Fan both the big toe and the little toe. While keeping them spread (you can hold them down with your hands), move the middle three toes first toward the big toe and then toward the little toe.

7) Hold the big toe down in the fanned position and draw all the other toes, including the little toe, toward it.

8) Hold the little toe down in the fanned position and draw all the other toes, including the big toe, toward it.

If your foot cramps at any time while exerting the tiny muscles of the foot, just stop and hold your foot or gently massage it until the cramp abates. Continue with half the effort of your previous attempt.

Your foot should now feel warm, relaxed, and articulated. Try walking around again. Do you feel more rolling action as you step from heel to toe? Do you feel less jarring of your bones as you step onto your foot? Do you feel a difference in the alignment of your leg? Can you feel a stronger push off? Is it easier to jump?

If you have been practicing everything suggested in this article, you may find that your feet feel very lively indeed. They are actually just as complex and articulated as your hands. There is, after all, considerable convenience in being able to turn off the bathtub water faucet without leaning forward, or of being able to give a massage using three "hands" at once. More important, however, is the fact that feet are truly our base of support. Their well-being is a prerequisite for locomotion. As it turns out, the major medical complaint of the elderly is not that their hearts or minds are failing (the major medical worry of their doctors). No, the elderly complain that their feet hurt. Caring for your feet might be the greatest gift you can give your body. Just remember that there is not just one way to use your feet correctly; they have at least two personas and probably a lot more.

The Upper Extremity:
Enfolding and Exposing

All the drawings for this article were sketched by my nondominant right hand. The "dream images" [fig. 1 and fig. 2] were completed by my untrained, nonjudgmental right hand. All the rest were finished by my more exacting left hand which can execute smooth straight and curved lines freehand.

A great master of the martial arts once dreamed that he had no arms. After that dream he was invincible. No one could beat him ever again in any form of combat.

A few years ago I recurrently dreamed that my "position of power" was one in which my body formed a front-side-out ring with my hands clasped around my ankles. Although this is a position of exposure, of total vulnerability, of no-handedness, it felt like a revelation of a profound secret source of endless energy and personal power for me. I would always wake from the dream with a strong sense of well-being.[fig. 1]

Somehow the fact that I have spent many of the most joyfully creative hours of my waking life curving around a cello or piano, or enfolded over a drawing or a student, [fig. 2] did not seem to conflict with my conviction in sleep that I must reach behind me to be truly filled with a sense of my life force. Like a medieval alchemist, I accepted the two self-images from day and night as necessary polarities coexistent in myself.

fig. 1—My dream "position of power."

45

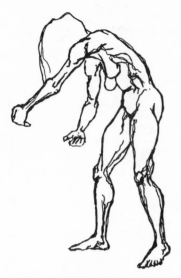

fig. 2—My waking posture of action.

Ever since that dream, I have found myself continuously practicing arm movements that involved arching my back and arms over the space behind me. I choreographed dances for the arms, swam hours of back stroke, and had my students draping over the backs of chairs with chests and throats opening to the ceiling. In fact I compulsively replicated my dream image.

Curious and wonderful things happened with these activities. The chronic back and neck spasms which had been a part of my life since childhood disappeared. Some of my students had similar relief. Going through the series of "arm dances" I created for myself always made me feel more energetic and responsive to the world around me no matter how depressed and tired I had been when I started the movements. This had repercussions. I felt that my teaching had taken a leap forward in its ability to communicate and to solve problems. I also found that I was becoming angry or upset with alarming frequency and I was totally unable to control my passionate responses, however inappropriate or inconvenient. In fact, I found myself screaming and yelling at people all the time. While I continued to feel brim full of lively energy, much of it was being expended in uncontrolled fits of fury.

Fearful, I began to curve my spine forward again, drawing my arms in across my chest. This seemed to immediately give me back my self control and calm acceptance of other people's human frailty. It also gave me back my neck spasms.

Now, in a real panic, I had no choice but to desperately seek help wherever I could get it, to listen to the very thing I told my students again and again: the solution to a functional problem lies always in the balance halfway between all the possible extremes.

Absurdly simple as the solution sounds, it is not simply achieved. I already knew that standing up straight as a board was only a way of sustaining my spasms more painfully. Dancers with perfectly correct spines and precisely held arms seemed to hold their breaths and their dynamics were bland and predictable.

Clearly, the balance between a hyperextending upper spine with arms reaching into the space behind and a flexing upper spine with arms pulled in to the front had to be a dynamic one. Somehow movement through all directions in space had to be taking place simultaneously for there to be a balance that doesn't hurt or dull.

In order to determine what the full range of movement to be balanced actually is in the upper extremity, one must first study the bone and joint structure in this part of the body, then test the muscles that move these bones to find what their actual functional capacity for contraction and stretch is, and finally go systematically through a gamut of upper extremity activities, noting the dynamic qualities with which they are performed as well as the space they circumscribe.

Since the potential range of motion of the upper extremity is tremendous, no one culture encourages the use of all this range in "normal" daily activity. Therefore, the final step involves performing movements one may have never thought of before. Performing activities that are "abnormal" may bring subtle censure from one's own internal, and perhaps uncompromising, moral judge. The censure may be in the form of feeling awkward or just uncomfortable with the unusual movements, or even a little sad or irritated.

Recognizing this internalized arbitrator's power helped solve a puzzle for me of why it is so difficult to find balance between extremes. If one extreme is judged "good" and the opposite "bad," then one can hardly feel balanced halfway between these two. Instead one will keep edging toward the "good" polarity. A further complication to this balancing problem is that the polarity that one consciously deems "good" may not be the one that feels good. In fact, early forgotten lessons or the magnificent mental etchings of dreams and visions can place a halo of desirability over the "bad" polarity and a haze of distress around the presumed "good."

Beside all this, human beings are uniquely gifted with a musculoskeletal system that allows enormous expression and manipulation of tools with the upper extremity. For this reason, we can never do random or "empty" arm movements. The passage of our hands through space seems to intrinsically carry meaning for ourselves and our world. While the meaning being conveyed varies infinitely for each one of us and in each environmental setting, the basic structure of bones and joints is shared by all of us. Let us now examine our common form.

The shoulder girdle is an incomplete bony ring composed of linked segments that rest on top of the rib cage. These four discretely movable parts consist of two clavicles (collar bones) in front and two scapulae (shoulder blades) in back. The scapulae are not jointed to each other or the trunk in back. The only junction between the shoulder girdle and the trunk itself is the connection at the base of our neck of the two clavicles with the top of the sternum (sternoclavicular joint). This arrangement of the shoulder girdle structure not only allows unihibited mobility of the thorax which it encircles, but it also permits isolation of right and left shoulder activity. Since the arms attach to the scapulae they gain the freedom of motion of the scapulae in relation to the trunk, in addition to that provided by the ball and socket structure of the shoulder joint proper (glenohumeral joint), in itself the most freely moveable joint in the body.

At the far end of the arm, our hand, mobilized and empowered from the shoulder, can reach just about any point on the surface of an imaginary sphere with approximately a three-foot radius from its axis, our chest. [fig. 3] A range of motion of 180 degrees at the

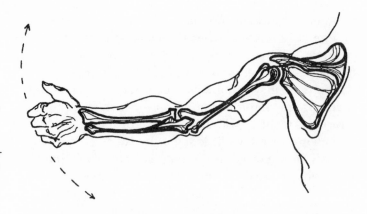

fig. 3—The movement of our scapula coupled with the movement of our shoulder joint allows us to reach almost any point on the surface of an imaginary sphere with approximately a three-foot radius from its axis at the center of our chest.

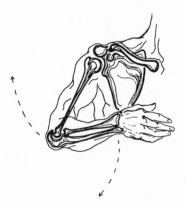

fig. 4—The range of motion at our elbow gives us the ability to touch almost any point, near or far, within the volume of our sphere of reach space.

elbow, midway between hand and shoulder, gives us the potential to touch almost any point within the volume of this same imaginary sphere. [fig. 4] The two bones that compose our forearm, the ulna and the radius, can rotate around each other so as to allow the palm of our hand to face all directions without change in the spatial orientation of the rest of our body.[fig. 5]

The hand itself is composed of twenty-seven small rounded bones that can move in relation to each other almost as easily and complexly as beach pebbles shifting under surf. [fig. 6] This facility within the hand's intrinsic skeletal composition, together with the large proportion of brain cortex given over to the orchestration of its functioning, gives the human being ability to touch or manipulate objects in space with a degree of coordination as fine as the eye can see, even under a microscope.[fig. 7]

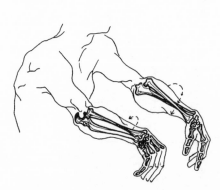

fig. 5—The bones of our forearm can rotate around each other, allowing the palm of our hand to face in all directions.

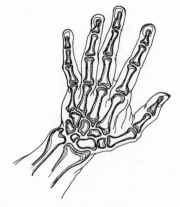

fig. 6—A view of the back of the hand showing twenty-six of the twenty-seven bones that form it. The last bone sits at the base of the palm on the little finger side. Therefore, it is only visible from a front view.

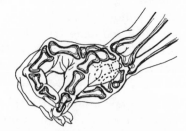

fig. 7—The fine-coordination of the human hand is made possible by the large area of brain cortex given over to the orchestration of its functioning. The fingertips and especially the thumbtip are very sensitive. Only human beings have the ability to bring all their fingertips together, as in this illustration. This is due to the unique proportions of the human hand.

fig. 8—A depiction of bringing my arm across the front of my body. Some of the muscles involved in producing this action are shown.

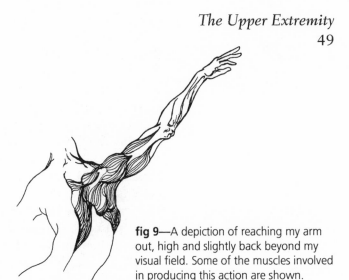

fig 9—A depiction of reaching my arm out, high and slightly back beyond my visual field. Some of the muscles involved in producing this action are shown.

The actual reach space that each one of us has at our command is frequently very much smaller than what I have just described. Many of us do not have either the flexibility or contractile strength of muscle needed to propel the bony levers of our arms through their full potential range of motion. The ability of muscles to contract and be stretched is only maintained through daily practice of movement that requires these abilities. If, for example, I work at a desk, kitchen counter, piano, or easel all day long, I am using the muscles that move my arms across the front of my body (flexors, adductors, and internal rotators of the shoulder)[fig. 8] a great deal more than the muscles which take my arms overhead or behind me, beyond my visual field (extensors, abductors and external rotators of the shoulder).[fig. 9] Unless I am a gymnast, my manual activities will take place from an upright sitting or standing position so that the same groups of muscles will be invariably working to counteract gravity, stabilizing my upper body against the activities of my arms. If my arms support and move a great deal of heavy weight every day, these antigravity muscles will be very strong and well-developed, but perhaps they will not be very flexible or speedy. They may somewhat sabotage a sudden choreographic urge to fling my arms like light, quick wings back and up behind me, while the muscles that must work to produce this action may be too "lazy" or weak to defy them.

The strength, flexibility, and fine-timing of contraction of one muscle relative to its antagonist, the muscle that causes opposing joint movement, is what determines not only the achievable movement range at a given joint but also the dynamic qualities of the movement through space, the "how" of the movement. This "textural" quality of touch serves us powerfully in communicating meaning to another person. Even when there is not contact between the fingertips of one person and the skin of another, the precise way in which hands caress the space around them transmits significance to the eyes of an audience. Dance would not be art if this were not so.

In order to voluntarily choose one's dynamics of touch, it is necessary to first neutralize any dynamics already implicit in the neuro-muscular patterns of rest or preparation to touch. This means giving up all extraneous muscle tension. While there are innumerable ways of doing this from any starting position, I like to begin by using visualization while lying down quietly. In my mind's eye I see my body as a marvelously shaped hollow vessel through which specific lines of movement pass just as water passes through pathways of a riverbed. The walls of the vessel form my body boundaries. The vessel itself is an adaptive receptacle. Its walls are extremely plastic, subject to the forces without and within it. Textured like a sieve, it allows exchange of substance with the atmosphere around it, continuously accommodating the pressures of movement by expanding or shrinking in size.

First I focus on my breath as if it were water flowing through me like a perpetually recycling fountain. As I inhale I imagine the water filling up my trunk so that I expand and grow with it in all directions. Then the exhalation shoots a spray of water up from the base of my pelvis through my central axis and out through the top of my head. This jet of water moves from my core in a clear unbroken stream so fine that it takes at least twice as long to complete an exhalation as it does to inhale.

The droplets of water that escape from the exhaled jet of fountain radiate a halo of mist around me. From the apex of the fountain the water falls down my face and neck, chest and arms in rivulets to earth, sometimes serpentine, sometimes straight, in the inevitable passage groundward. Then before emptiness becomes stillness, the cycle of breath curves round to begin again with the growth of my inhalation.

If my rib cage seems still not to have enough space or movement inside of it, I may visualize each rib circle as a horizontal gaseous ring, fluid as the rings of Jupiter. As I inhale, the bright gases flow from my sternum out along each rib to my sides, continuing to flow, as I exhale, over each rib all the way to its attachment to my spine in back. Here the fingers of flowing gas join to form a pool of light within my spinal column, in the very centers of the vertebral bodies. As I inhale again, the illuminated gas bursts through my chest and radiates out from my sternum along my ribs to continue their circuit, slightly enlarged from the first time. [fig. 10]

Having expanded my thorax in all dimensions, I think now of my shoulder blades melting open from my rib cage. I see my scapulae as wings which can unfold so that their lower tips move apart, away from my spine, toward my armpits, and out into the air on either side of my body, as in fig. 9. Simultaneously, the distance between my shoulder joints increases, as if my shoulders were radiating outward from the base of my thorax, at the level of my twelfth thoracic vertebra.

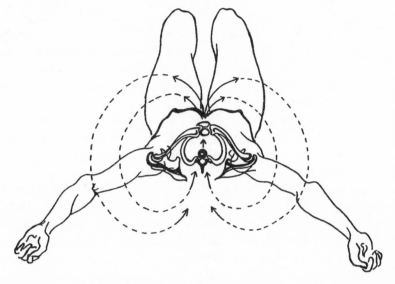

fig. 10—An overhead view of the first rib circle surrounded by the shoulder girdle. The arrows and dotted lines represent my imagining of a series of gaseous rings traveling from the front of my sternun, out beyond the sides of my ribs, around to the back of my thoracic vertebrae, and finally through my chest to return to the front of my sternum. With each breath cycle, the rings grow larger.

With shoulders grown wide to the sides, I start to think of a light source being generated at the center of my chest (at the level of the seventh thoracic vertebra approximately where the heart is located). This ball of light sends out its beams to my shoulder joints. Instead of thinking of the joints in the body anatomically, as one bone meeting another bone, I imagine my joints as gateways which I can open to the light. As the beam of light from my chest passes through the now open gateway

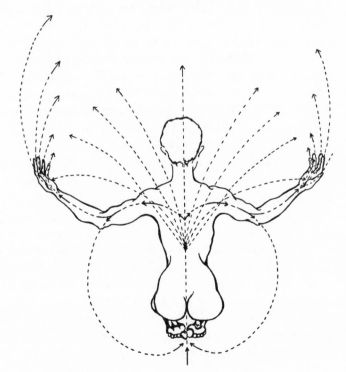

fig. 11—A back view of a visualization of light radiating from the area of the twelfth thoracic vertebra and the seventh thoracic vertebra, through the shoulders, elbows, wrists, palms, and out through each fingertip into the space beyond.

at my shoulder joints, it enlarges the space within the joint in the process of shining through it. The beam of light (like the river of blood pumping through my veins) continues through the internal space of my elbow joint, wrist, center of my palm, and out through the tips of each finger into the space around and beyond me, gradually curving back to earth to become a potential source of future energy. [fig. 11]

Perhaps when I stand I will think of connecting to earth's potential energy, taking it in through the soles of my feet, receptive as infants' eyes, up into my legs, pelvis, spine, thorax and out again through my shoulders, arms, hands and fingertips.

The patterns of the past that my muscles have codified into rigidly held joint positions and characteristic gestures have been emptied out of me, "neutralized." As I stand, my dynamic response to the next moment of my future can be freely chosen rather than habitual.

If I am touching someone else I will be able to feel their textures and the forces moving within them, instead of just the pressure of my own tight-held fingers indenting their skin. Something is exchanged through our nerve endings and we are both moved by each other. Each one of us experiences a slight rearrangement of all our cells. New sensations, more complex patterns from waves colliding are born. If what comes to me from contact with another person seems undesirable to me at any time, I can simply allow it to continue its movement quickly and unimpeded out of me through the very same pathways from my body to earth that I opened wide during my visualization activity. Indeed, I have been led to the conviction that this completely unresistant "open" quality of joints is what made the tai chi master invulnerable after his dream of having no arms. His arms became so receptive, so neutral, that they had no character of their own. As a result he was able to respond fully and accurately to any and all actions of his opponent, serving only as a conduit for all the blows that were then harmlessly grounded. Needless to say, facing another living organism (under any circumstances, not just those of life and death combat) is almost, but not quite, impossible to do with total neutrality and openness, without any use of previously learned techniques or defensive contraction.

From my experience with myself and my students, I soon found that the challenge of maintaining unblocked flow is not the same for the right and the left arms. Each arm has its own fluid dynamics. Each arm has a distinct personality with its own activity preferences and skills, ways of sensing and manipulating the world.

During the progress of a course I taught on the upper extremity in the spring of 1979, my students and I found that we didn't each have a dominant hand and a receptive one (that could perhaps excel at tai chi). The situation was not that simple. Each hand was aggressive or skilled for particular but different areas of "smartness" and "stupidity." Each hand "saw" reality in its own way.

When we drew ourselves with one hand and then with the other, we created portraits of two very different people. In fact, the figures I drew with my nondominant hand were far more mysteriously beautiful and delicately detailed, far more delightful to my eyes than the figure I sketched with my dominant well-trained hand. Systematically going through a list of myriad activities first with one hand and then with the other, we each found previously hidden skills and movement qualities in ourselves. Letting the "nondominant" hand initiate movement stimulated choreographic ideas that had never occurred to us before. While finding new choreographic sources had not been a goal in the class, it certainly was a major side effect.

The oddest and most unexpectedly powerful repercussion of our explorations in the class was a tremendous outburst of dreaming which continued even after the course had formally ended. Everyone's dreams were wildy varied but all were in vivid color, kinesthetically lucid, intensely physical, and not like anything the person had ever dreamed before. In the dreams we had arms powerful as mountains, delicate as dewed ferns turned to gold in the sunlight, soaring and twisting up and out with the lush voluptuousness of tropical plants magically transforming light into growth.

Taking Root to Fly:
The Human Spine

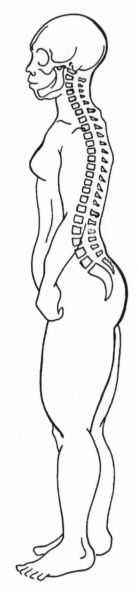

fig. 1—A side view of the vertebral column

O nce I imagined myself to be a creature with enormous wings empowered to move on the fulcrum of a rigid spine. At first, the idea of flight by means of the liquidity of wings was delicious. But then I started to think of the large still structure at my core that supposedly allowed me to soar through celestial spheres. If my spine were actually a solid vertical column, how would my daily life be affected?

My head could only face in one direction—the one I was already traveling in. I would not be able to look down at my own body, above me, or to either side. While I could still breathe, there would not be the reserve allowed by springlike action in the thoracic spine, the part of the spine to which the ribs attach. The length of my stride as I shifted into walking, running, or leaping would be limited to the range of motion possible at my hip joints alone, for my pelvis would be fused to the pillar of my trunk. This last realization: that all distinct pelvic movement would be lost to me, was what turned my whimsy into nightmare. What are heavenly delights of flying when earthly ones are withdrawn?

Such a fantasy of spinal solidity is apparently not unique to me. I work with an elegantly beautiful woman who has labored successfully to maintain a plumb-line-like back. If one is rewarded in heaven for achieving godlike erectness, then she will be repaid for her efforts in full. During her mortal life, however, she suffers severe neck pain. The constantly contracting muscles that have held her rigorous posture have also applied such compression stress on her vertebrae over the years that her x-rays show them to have grown arthritic in response. Ironically, her only relief from pain comes when she is dancing.

Human beings are designed to move. With our spines perpendicular to earth, rather than parallel to it, we are only anchored to the ground by our lower end, our pelvis and legs. Using the lower limbs as a base, our spines can coil and uncoil elastically through space, lending our arms power and range, our eyes the ability to view the entire sphere of light around us, our pelvis and legs interaction with the earth.

The "still point at the center of the dance" is bone: the fulcrum of movement, the axis of rotation. However, the spine as a whole is not a still point. It consists of twenty-five moveable bone segments, plus the head which is a kind of crowning giant vertebra. [fig. 1]

A teacher of mine once suggested that these vertebrae balance like twenty-six stacked china teacups. If you trust yourself not to be clumsy, such an image allows the vertebrae to align themselves so that minimal muscle work is required to maintain them there, against the pull of gravity. [figs. 2, 3, and 4]

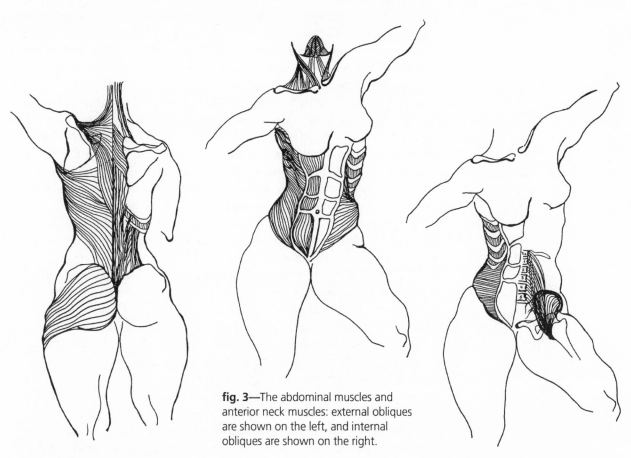

fig. 3—The abdominal muscles and anterior neck muscles: external obliques are shown on the left, and internal obliques are shown on the right.

fig. 2—The muscles of the back: superficial layers are shown on the left; a deeper layer is shown on the right.

fig. 4—The transversus abdominus—the deepest layer of the abdominal wall—is shown on the left, and the deeper iliopsoas muscle is shown on the right.

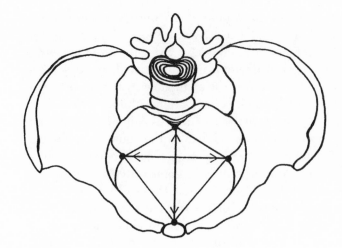

fig. 5—A view from above through the pelvis to the pelvic floor.

I have created more dramatic imaginary supports for myself in the flight heavenward. Some of these visualizations came from teachers and students who have given me generous feedback. Other visualizations come from my own dreaming, both in sleep and in the process of concentrated movement practice.

One of these involves visualizing my pelvis from the inside. It is a funnel of bone with a diamond-shaped base. The four points of the base are as follows. The pubic symphysis, a prominence halfway between the hip joints, forms the front. The coccyx, little "tail" bones that attach to the end of the sacrum which is itself the lower end of the spine, forms the back. The ischial tuberosities, "sitting bones," form the two sides. I think of this diamond shape expanding and sinking, glowing like an incandescent light. [fig. 5]

As this basin of light becomes more and more brilliant, millions of rays of light shoot straight up from it through the front of my spine into my skull, into my brain, and out through the top of my head. The rays beam through my trunk, through all my abdominal organs, my diaphragm, my chest, through my heart and lungs, through my neck and all of my larynx, pharynx, and vocal apparatus to the root of my tongue, my mouth, my sinuses and nose, my eye sockets, and all the spaces of my face. The light of my pelvis, like an oil lamp, illuminates my entire body and the space around me.

I think of each beam of light as a thread moving straight as an arrow shot sunward. All the light threads move together but each is distinctly separate and so silky that it can sway without breaking.

Sometimes I imagine that instead of light, there is a lake in the bed of my pelvic floor. Beneath the lake is a fissure in the earth through which volcanic fire erupts. Meeting the water in the lake, the fire creates steam that sends a geyser out of the once mirror-calm surface of the lake, out through the center of my torso, and up through the top of my head, leaving a sunlit veil of spray all around my body.

Occasionally the fire evaporates the lake altogether and burns white heat out of my eyeballs and fingertips.

Be it light, fire, or water that surges up the central axis, the glow, sparks, or foam that it generates can unfold the core out, expanding the body boundaries in all directions. Eddies from the fountain make bubbles, air spaces between the bones where each vertebra articulates with the next one. The ripples make muscles release their stranglehold on bone. Little streams slip between the layers and layers of muscle and connective tissue giving each muscle cell breathing room. Dew soaks into the skin and expands it into air's caress. This expansion outward prevents the tall column of spine from collapsing back into itself.

On occasion the realities of daily life don't seem to nurture thoughts of columns of light or fire. The internal dialogue insists on sagittal narrowness, on compulsive attention to concrete mechanical problems. Under these circumstances my mind can only be focused on precise and repetitive plane geometry. Thus led, I systematically construct series of diamonds and triangles in the three planes of my body.

I imagine three diamond-shaped bases or "floors" in the horizontal plane, parallel with the ground. The lowest diamond is formed by connecting points from the centers of the two hip joints to points in the sacrum and the pubic symphysis. [fig. 6] The middle diamond is formed by connecting points from the centers of the two shoulder joints to points in the upper sternum (manubrium) and the back of the second thoracic vertebra. [fig. 7] The upper diamond is formed by connecting points from the bones just below the two ears (mastoid processes) to the midlines of the base of the skull in back (occipital bone) and the

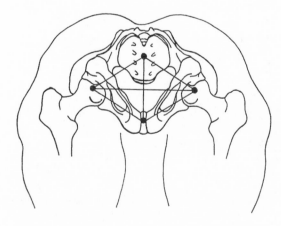

fig. 6—A view of the pelvis and hips from below, showing the diamond formed by connecting points from the two hip joints to points in the sacrum and the pubic symphysis.

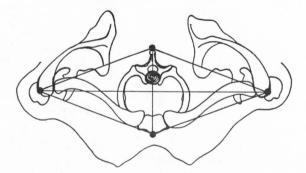

fig. 7—A view of the shoulder girdle from above, showing the diamond formed by connecting points from the two shoulder joints to points in the sternum and the posterior spinous process of the second thoracic vertebra.

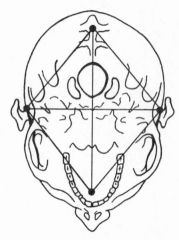

fig. 8—A view, of the skull from below, showing the diamond formed by connecting points from just below the two ears to points on the occiput and the hard palate.

hard palate in front (maxilla). [fig. 8] If I visualize increasing the distance between the front and back points of each diamond—resulting in more space between pubic symphysis and sacrum, sternum and thoracic vertebra, hard palate and occiput—I may enhance sagittal motion in such activities as walking, running, and seeing into the distance. If I also visualize increasing the distance between the paired side points—hip joints, shoulder joints, ears—I may enhance coronal/frontal motion in actions like shifting my weight from foot to foot, side stepping and reaching, or listening carefully with my ears. When I increase the distance between all the points, I may experience expansion of the horizontal dimension, affording me greater ease in rotating to either side.

Focus on the lowest diamond's expansion might yield greater stability of my pelvis and lower spine. Consideration of the middle diamond's expansion can afford me greater mobility of my arms through space. Attention to the upper diamond's expansion may give me the sense of greater perceptual adaptability, both visual and auditory. When I encompass all three diamonds at once, I notice that the median frontal plane of my body bisects the sides—hip joints, shoulder joints, ears—of all three. [fig. 9]

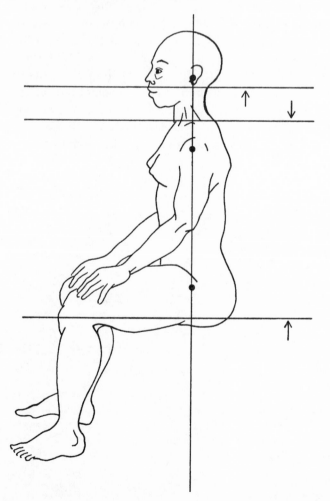

fig. 9—The vertical line on the figure represents the edge of the median frontal (coronal) plane. The horizontal lines indicate the locations of the cross-sectional views shown in the horizontal diamonds visualized in the pelvis, shoulder girdle, and skull.

Shifting my orientation into the median frontal plane, by looking into the mirror I see that I can draw diagonals in my mind from right hip joint to left shoulder, left shoulder to right ear; and from left hip joint to right shoulder, right shoulder to left ear. The lower diagonals cross each other at approximately my twelfth thoracic vertebra—which is the pivot vertebra between my thoracic and lumbar spine. The upper diagonals cross at approximately my third cervical vertebra—behind my hyoid bone (attachment for my tongue muscles) and thyroid carti-lage (Adam's apple). Now, I have constructed a triangle-shaped space between my two hip joints and my twelfth thoracic vertebra. I have a diamond-shaped space contained between my twelfth thoracic, my two shoulder joints, and my third cervical vertebra. On top, I have a trian-gle-shaped space standing on its apex which is formed by the connec-tions between the third cervical vertebra and my ears. [fig. 10]

When I imagine that the lowest triangle is growing, I feel more "rooted." When I imagine that the middle diamond is enlarging, I feel "winged." As I imagine that the upper triangle is expanding, I feel as if I can hear and be heard as I sing out from the resonating cavern of my throat and mouth.

Sometimes I tend to visualize these geometries from a front view. However, instead of only thinking of the part of my body that I can actually see, I imagine that all the cells on the back surface of my body are eyes seeing into a mirror behind me that reflects me from my heels to the ends of the hair on my head.

To maximize my sense of volume, I can think that every cell in my body is able to "see" in all directions: inward and outward, side-ways and center, upward and downward, as well as forward and backward. By the time I am "seeing" thus, my mind's obsession with mundane and tightly held perceptions is dispersed.

But, with my violently dramatic imagination unleashed, irra-tional fears of spinal instability don't necessarily disappear. On the contrary, they may actually increase. With a circumference enlarged in all dimensions, far beyond the dictates of fashion, I become fear-ful that the whole pillar of fire will take off into the cosmic void leaving nothing behind but the flaccid remains of skin and toenails in a tiny heap. This terror, not assuaged by an elementary working knowledge of physics, provides reinforcement to a tendency to hun-ker: hunch the back, grip buttocks under like a dog, and grasp the unresponsive floor with all ten toes. While hunkering gives me a sense of kinesthetic kinship with Victorian furniture, I feel the need to search further for a sense of certainty that I will not be uprooted by my own self-help efforts.

Returning to the fire-under-the-lake idea, I remind myself that if the lake basin is my pelvis, then the fire must come up from the earth through the passageway of my two legs via the gateway of my feet. That the fire does shoot steam or flame through the lake is

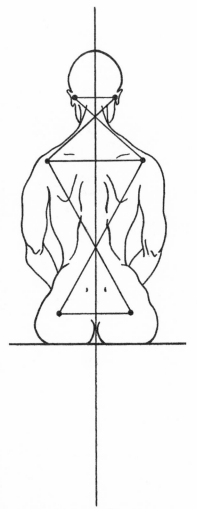

fig. 10—A view of the back of the body. Lines have been drawn to connect the right hip joint to the left shoulder joint to the right ear. Lines have also been drawn to connect the left hip joint to the right shoulder joint to the left ear. Paired points have also been connected. The diagonals cross the spine at aproximately the twelfth tho-racic vertebra and the third cer-vical vertebra.

proof an open channel of connection to the depth of the earth exists. If the earth-rootedness is lost, then there will be no jet stream of fire upward either. I also note that the more the fire spews skyward from the volcano, the more massive is the supporting mountain remaining once the eruption is over. Volcanic ash does fly on the wind, but more solid mountain remains behind melted firmly into earth by the lava that oozes down it, black as swamp mud.

A wise teacher described to me the kinesthetic experience of this melting into earth. She spoke of the sensation as "a peasant digging for potatoes, barely breaking rhythm to give birth in the fresh-turned dirt." In rooting thus, however, one doesn't drain away energy but rather gains a child or potatoes at the least.

One need not pull the pelvis down and dig in with heels and toes in an effort to plant oneself. It is enough to let the water rain into the lake (abdominal contents fall into the pelvis), the lake sit in the lake bed on the mountain (pelvis sits on the heads of the femurs or thigh bones), the mountain sides slide to earth (the thigh muscles and calf muscles melt down along the femur and tibia of each leg to the feet), the fissures under the mountain that lead to earth's molten core remain open (the soles of the feet spread and open to the ground as if they were eyes looking through water).

As if there were no skin at all between feet and fertile earth, the root finds you as it wells up from the depth seeking sunlight.

In a dream, I experienced this "root" from the earth as a giant woman of fire resembling me exactly in every detail except size. I inhaled her flaming breath through my feet. When it reached my pelvis, it mixed with my own breath with such turbulence that blue-red heat was generated which expanded and empowered my whole body. The excess poured out the top of my head and back down to earth for another cycle. The dream reassured me that the energy source I was drawing from, the gargantuan woman, was unlimited. I could not float away like a helium-filled balloon since any energy I inhaled into me through my feet eventually exhaled back out of me into earth again. This unbroken circuit itself bound me to earth.

Comforting though it was, this first dream was not enough to change my usual waking way of seeing. Going up into the Rocky Mountains with my teacher one day, I found out just how different our perceptions were. My eyes were constantly raised to admire the top of the mountains, where the sky silhouettes the jagged peaks. My teacher's attention was on the mass of the mountain itself so that she marvelled at its vast base, its profound strong root.

That night I dreamed that I repeatedly stood at the top of a children's slide and looked down it, then slid, head first, fearlessly down. Looking and sliding down until it was familiar habit felt like an essential practice. Fear, I already knew, had made me close my eyes, hold my breath, my ribs, my shoulders, hold my fists tightly far away from the ground.

In the next dream, fingers of light sent shining rivers along each rib until my entire rib cage melted down into my pelvis which expanded to embrace all. As the need to defend myself departed, my spine uncoiled.

The Dark Side of the Brain:
Working with the Dynamics of Touch Through the Nondominant Hand

These drawings and stories were made in the process of a course I taught in the fall of 1979. I was trying to make conscious a number of the unconscious aspects of my teaching work for my students, the aspects that I had previously called "intuitive." As I began to use my previously nondominant right hand to draw and write with I became aware of dynamics to my work that had previously been unknown to me. I also began to have a better sense of three-dimensional spatial orientation as well as less fear of getting lost in that space. My movement became freer. Students who were right-handed had similar experiences drawing with their left hands. The stories were written over a period of two weeks just before going to sleep; they are entirely unedited. I am still not ready to draw conclusions and my right hand is not as anxious about this as my left hand would normally be.

A Story Written with the Right Hand

Once upon a space between two or three molecules, there grew a beam of light. It had traveled long and far from a deep sea mountain covered with red plant-fish and coral. Dappling and sparkling up from blackness into green and blue and finally white water it became thinner and denser as it flew until it entered an eye.

The egg of vision thus fertilized caressed by the optic nerves so gently that it slept was carried deep into the brain's caverns, large as

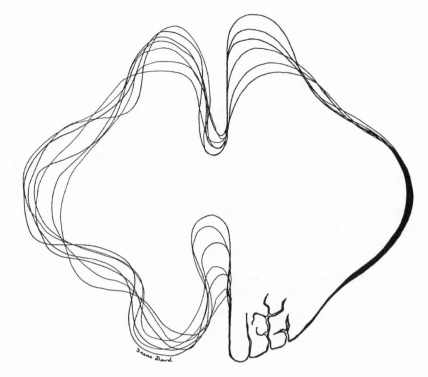

View from above of the cerebral hemispheres of a left-handed, right-hemispheric dominant person, myself. My left hand drew the right brain and my right hand drew the left brain.

mountains. The egg's dream illuminated the walls of the cave showing crystalline forms perfect as snow, revealing other beings too thick and complicated to even remember or see. The egg was embraced by these however and remembered their touch.

The egg of vision was not frightened even though it never came to rest and never saw with the same dream twice. Mystery clothed strangeness with soft robes that the egg child loved to grasp and chew. Swallowing the juices that flowed all colors from the mystery robes the infant laughed.

This very laughter shook a dolphin from her sleep. Where has my child gone? the mother cried from her sea mountain. Swimming deeper and deeper a spiral, she found only black smooth silence and not her child of light. Weeping in the night a dolphin mother is invisible to the mind's eye. Blue-grey her lovely flanks in sunlight now have no color. They are visible only to an ear.

Grief gives the dolphin wisdom and she plays her lute softly and quickly until the ear awakes to hear her call its name. "AUR, AUR!" the dolphin's lute calls. This is the ear's favorite most secret name. When ear hears its name called so blue and grey it leaps out quickly dancing its best dance.

Of course when the child of vision, the beam of light sees the dancing of the ear it cannot resist. Light dances gold until it fills the brain to bursting. Brain, thinking it is sun now arcs slowly down, down to the light. The dolphin can just barely reach brain with her spout of water and takes her baby ever so gently down her spout just exactly like sunlight down a waterfall. Brain remembers.

Brain was taking a walk one day when suddenly it remembered that once it had been an oak tree. If its coronal radiations were the branches then obviously its cerebral cortex was the leaves and acorns. But where was the trunk and roots?

Brain surveyed the world around itself. It was surrounded by space. Below was the sea playing with the wind. Brain couldn't see wind but it saw light on the water doing wind dancing. Also ear was dancing to wind music. Above the sun shown down on the water.

Brain understood now Brain was Sun. Hadn't brain nurtured the egg of vision? Hadn't the light egg exploded gold cascading into a Mother dolphin's head fountain?

The river of light from sun into sea must be the tree trunk. The dolphin must be the roots and the sea root's soil.

Brain felt happy now that all was clear. Brain was not disturbed that the sun stood above it. Was not the fact that brain saw sun and felt so like sun fully proof enough that it was sun?

Entranced brain began to trace the sun's root threads from sky to

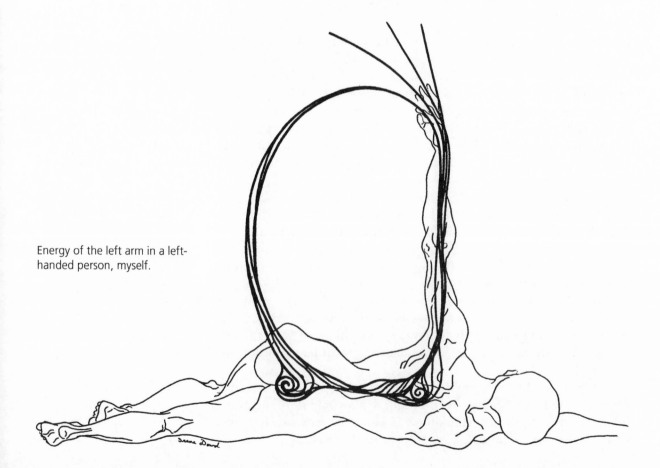

Energy of the left arm in a left-handed person, myself.

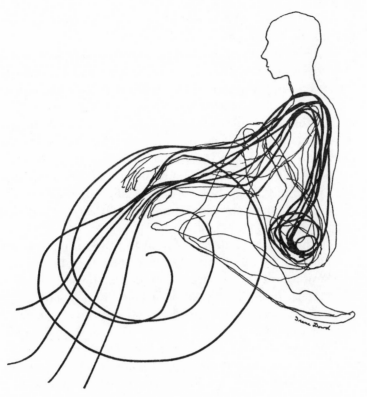

My right hand drawing the way
I use my energy when I am
involved in teaching through
touch.

the base of the mountain under the sea. Brain had never noticed
them before. They were very fine and translucent to every color. They
moved with the slightest breath of wind and yet they never broke.

As brain systematically followed each thread from sun molecule to
sea ground, it noticed that some threads shimmered in the other
direction: from sea floor to sun. Every single sun molecule had a
thread connection to sea-ground and every single molecule of earth at
sea bottom had a thread connection to sun. Having followed the
opposing directions of so many threads brain realized that it no longer
knew if sun or sea was above or below it or if one were the other.

This was a frightening thought. If a tree is uprooted will it not
die of shock and starvation? Brain began to turn pale and tremble at
the idea. Alas, I die!

Weeping and moaning, brain began to lose consciousness. Brain
saw neither sun light or sea dark. Brain felt itself expanding, dissi-
pating, falling, falling. . . .

Ah ha! If I am falling then the direction I am going is down,
below me towards the center of the earth below the sea floor. That
means I know where I am!

That means I will soon be at the center of the world at the very
end of down. As brain fell the sides of mountains flew up to its left
and trees on the mountains changed shape to ones more shadowy

and hugely heavy. Wind fell with brain just for fun, nudging brain toward the mountain every now and then.

Falling faster and faster brain wondered if it would fall further than the center of the earth. What would it feel like there? Like roots? Like a subterranean cave river bed? How do rivers feel?

Filled with questions brain tried to close its eyes to keep them out. At that moment brain hit the shore sand and bounced.

At the moment of impact, brain felt itself grow short as a mushroom and just as wide. Ugh! What dreadful shape I'm in. Must—

Suddenly brain felt the earth thrust up like a volcano and brain was soaring off like—like nothing at all. No shape, no direction, no threads, just the light that had danced in the threads. Brain was so bedazzled it forgot to think.

At the instant that brain forgot to think, the moon rose up from her bath engulfing all with her wet body, translucently perfect as a newborn infant skin, each vein a blue visible tree.

Moon's smile is so yielding it eats brain in one swallow whole. Brain doesn't notice that now it is only root, totally body of the moon. Brain isn't thinking even more than when it stopped thinking. Moon was always too busy to think. Sun did all the thinking for her, thinking words like "up" and "down" and "I am up above the sea down below." Brain isn't Sun any more. Brain isn't. There is only moon.

Moon spirals so that wind blows her all dry from her bath. Now moon is ready for dinner. Shooting a beam from her eye, she hooks a lion with it. After moon draws it in, she quaffs her prey as wine from a cup. Thank you, her tongue dances, thank you her throat, her aesophagus, her stomach, her blood cells sing. Moon thanks her cells for singing.

Some cells of moon are brain rippled and splashed throughout her. These cells are brain color. They call out their shades in harmony. They like to sing eight voice fugues: from cuboid bone—foot's fountain, from the root of the third metacarpal, from acetabulum and glenoid fossa, from sacrum, sternum, occiput and sella turcica. Each cell echoes and vibrates into its bone, the space in and around its bone— warming the marrow, melting it into rivulets that trickle quiet and booming as secrets in the corridors where cells breathe. Moon herself dances in these corridors of breath where moonbeams fly forever past the saddle of the universe's face and back again inside out.

These are moon's smile, sun's silence, brain's roots. Unremembered.

A Story Written with the Left Hand—A Continuation of the Story for the Right Hand

Moon is the most ancient goddess of the solar system since she was last to become visible. Carrying her scythe on her left side, she strides everywhere in her robes made of mountains and leopards darkness.

She protects life by killing to feed her own loveliness, by slicing away all that has neither red or green in it. Thus, the tapestry of veins grows.

By reason of her cutting edge, although no victim sees the line of a blade, left is called sinister and female and bloody in one hard breath.

On one side of the blade is the solar wind caressing moon's craters, on the other side is the fullness of moon's flesh radiating the no light which fills the spaces between the stars. There is no gap between.

Moon's sisters are dark clouds too huge to identify. Their dance is slower than trees growing, than the earth dying, but it is very fine. A single molecule's sarabande fills the thousand mile gap between.

Moon's dance, by contrast, is very dense, all inside herself. Root and soil do combat with water but all of them clasp air in the end. This is the difference between moon and earth: in earth two elements do not share the same breath.

One day moon decided to take her bath outside. She loves baths and takes at least two a day. Since all the solar system is her home,

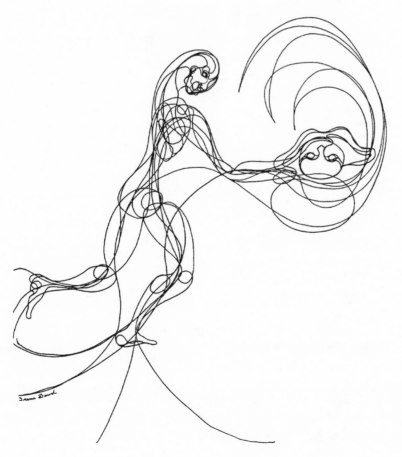

My left hand drawing the way I use my energy when I am involved in teaching through touch.

and she can take a bath in any room she pleases, she doesn't step through the door to go outside.

In order to be outside she curls herself up into a ball so large that—UAH! suddenly she is playing with her sisters the dark clouds in the pools and streams outside the milky way.

These pools and streams run everywhere inside brain as they are brain's roots, even though brain likes to call them "my body" or "my flesh." Of course brain only is concerned about these namings when at the moments of coming out of dreaming. It is at these moments only when brain feels itself solidifying and feels the need to know rocks. All other times, the pools and streams flow namelessly everywhere and everynowhere.

9

On Metaphor

M etaphor can be the fist that breaks through the dark glass between what is already known and what is still mystery.

Through the vehicle of metaphor, we can participate in that *movement* from what *is* to what *can be*.

Once in the new land on the other side of the dark glass, we can use the metaphor as a landmark from which to foray into the new world.

Eventually the metaphor dissipates in explosion outward from its core into the space of new landscape. Finally another metaphor coils around the landscape, coalescing into a new vehicle in which we continue the journey.

*

At one time I was working with two students who both experienced almost constant neck pain and stiffness. Although they each had what was considered to be exemplary posture, both of them appeared to hold their necks and heads rigidly in that posture even when all the rest of their body was moving. While they were able to voluntarily move their necks and heads, the movement was simply to another holding position that also caused pain. Soon, I also noticed that their eyes seemed to hold still with the same dynamics that their heads did. Perhaps, I hypothesized, if their eyes could begin to move smoothly and continuously, the muscles in their necks could begin to soften and "unfreeze" although no painful neck movements were being risked. I suggested that each student practice the following series of movements, both actual and imagined, while I observed and guided them.

While lying supine so that the backs of their heads were supported by the ground or a small pad on the ground, I asked that they move their eyes at random in all directions including: up and down, side to side, clockwise and counterclockwise. If strain was experienced, the range and intensity of movement was decreased by half. Then I asked my students to close their eyes gently. I reminded them that eyeballs are large globes floating in deep sockets of bone. Now, instead of having them actually turn their eyeballs to look in various directions, I asked them to visualize their eyeballs as spheres growing to expand into various spatial dimensions. I asked both students to imagine their eyeballs expanding downward toward their feet to fill the spaces at the bases of their skulls, then to imagine their eyeballs expanding upward toward the tops of their heads to fill the spaces at their crowns. Next, both imagined oscillating between the expansion downward and the expansion upward at a comfortable speed, neither agitatedly rapid nor stressfully slow. Having established a sense of motion in this dimension, they could then explore another dimension. Next, both students imagined their eyeballs expanding inward to fill the space all the way to their noses, then outward to fill the space all the way to their ears. An easy oscillation between noses and ears was established. Finally, both imagined their eyeballs growing in a third dimension. Their eyeballs grew backward to fill the backs of their skulls resting on the ground, and then grew forward to fill the spaces under their eyelids exposed to the sky. They pictured their eyeballs growing alternately back into their skulls/ ground and forward into their eyelids/sky in a regular rhythm.

As I went through these visualizations with both of my students, I found that their neck muscles were not as tight, seemed to "breathe" more under my "listening" fingers. The muscles seemed to actually be "breathing" in time with their imagined eye oscillations. Both students claimed to be "more relaxed." However, there was also a significant difference in the response of one in contrast to the response of the other.

The first student could easily visualize an expansion of her eyeballs into the front space under her eyelids, but this imaginary action made her uncomfortable and sometimes increased her pain. She had great difficulty, however, in even thinking about the space in the back of her skull much less imagining her eyeballs expanding into that space toward the ground. The second student found that thinking of his eyeballs sinking toward the back of his skull was simple, painful, and almost automatic. In fact, his thoughts seemed to be already there habitually. Picturing the space in front of his eyes, or a movement of his eyes into the space ahead of him was another matter altogether. Such a goal was vague and elusive in his thoughts, and all his powers of concentration were challenged in order to achieve it even momentarily.

When the first student stood up again, we talked about the session. I noticed that while she listened to me, her eyes seemed to reach out to me, appearing to bulge luminously toward me in a wide-eyed stare. When I asked how she was feeling, she told me that, yes, the pain had returned after its merciful remission while lying down. Mentioning my observation, I suggested we experiment with thinking of her eyes sinking back into their sockets, rather than reaching out, as she continued to converse with me. She complied readily but soon became agitated. She said that thinking of her eyes in this manner made her feel very removed from me, far away, as if she wasn't really listening at all. Even though I noted that my experience was in contrast to hers, that I felt that she now looked more receptive to my communication with her, she could not be persuaded or reassured. She insisted that she could not bear the sensation of not-looking at me and not-paying-attention to me that she had when she let her eyes be cradled in their sockets. After discussion and experimentation on her part in her daily life, we concluded that for her, "looking" and "seeing" were processes that involved reaching out with her eyes as if to grasp the light waves.

When the second student stood up, I asked him to walk around the room as he talked with me. As he ambled, I saw that he was automatically doing what was so fearful for the first student. Although his voice was warm and responsive, his eyes seemed glassy. It was as if his real, seeing eyes had sunk so far back into his head that what I saw on the surface of his face was just a transparent skin, a thick protective membrane to his eyes. In response to my questioning, he explained that he understood "looking" and "seeing" as a passive receiving of light waves into his retinas, a sort of waiting for the light waves to soak into his skull like water into soil.

Given the extreme contrast in the models of visual perception these two articulate students had taught me, I formulated a third model. I supposed that seeing is an activity in which one is simultaneously both reaching out for light and receiving light with the organs of vision. Delighted with my little yin/yang synthesis, I spent months in an orgy of visualizing every part of the body as a seeing eye: each vertebra of the spine, the pelvis, the rib cage, the entire trunk as a whole— all of these could be eyes seeking light and being illuminated by it.

Eventually, the obvious question occurred to me: how *do* we actually see? I began to reason in my best simple-minded and con-cretistic fashion. If it is true that "form follows function," then an examination of the dynamic process of the development of the eye from embryo to seeing child should give me some insight into the dynamics of adult human vision. First, I looked at the form of the embryonic human nervous system of which the optic nerves are a part. [fig. 1 and 2]

After much perusal of developmental anatomy, I sought further simplification through the depiction/description of the developmental process in five arbitrarily determined stages. [fig. 3]

fig. 1—A side view of the neural tube (primitive central nervous system of the embryo) at 28 days. An arrow indicates the optic vesicles or bulbs.

fig. 2—A front view of the head end of the neural tube at 28 days. An arrow indicates the optic vesicles or bulbs.

fig.3—Stages of "seeing."

Stages of development of the human eye

Metaphorical model

STAGE 1—28-day-old embryo: The optic vesicles protrude from the head end of the neural tube toward the surface ectoderm (primitive skin, the interface between the inside and outside world of the embryo).

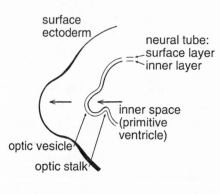

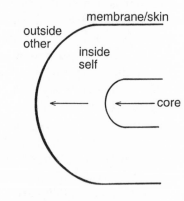

STAGE 2—30-day-old embryo: As the optic vesicles or bulbs continue to grow outward from the neural core, they become concave, cupping as if to receive the outside world they approach (these optic cups are the primitive retina, ground for the light sensitive rods and cones). Stimulated by the approach of the optic cups, surface ectoderm begins to thicken and invaginate into the cups.

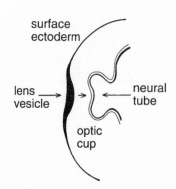

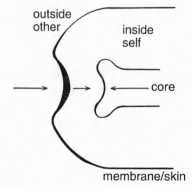

fig.3 *continued*

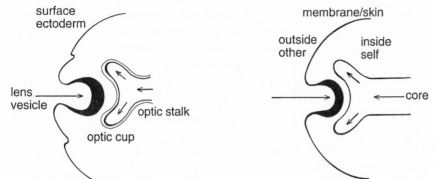

surface ectoderm

lens vesicle

optic stalk

optic cup

membrane/skin

outside other

inside self

core

STAGE 3—33-day-old embryo:
The optic cups continue to enlarge, encircling and grasping the thickened surface ectoderm. As if the optic cups were inhaling it, the surface ectoderm continues to grow into the cups until it has itself inhaled, encircled tiny globes of the outside world (these globes are the primitive lens, which will be able to change shape to accommodate vision from things far to things near in the outside world, just as if still remembering that outer place).

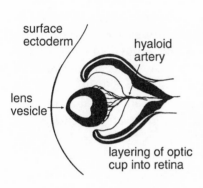

surface ectoderm

hyaloid artery

lens vesicle

layering of optic cup into retina

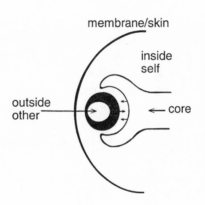

membrane/skin

inside self

outside other

core

STAGE 4—42-day-old embryo:
Immediately filaments grow to join each optic cup (continuous with the neural core) with each lens vesicle (bubble of outside other). These filaments provide a rudimentary blood supply called the hyaloid artery which nurtures the rapidly differentiating and growing primitive eye (this is gradually replaced by the circulatory system that is fully mature at eight months).

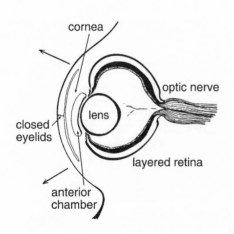

cornea

optic nerve

lens

closed eyelids

layered retina

anterior chamber

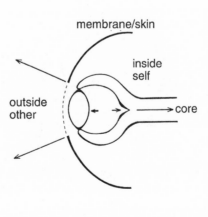

membrane/skin

inside self

outside other

core

STAGE 5—100-day-old embryo:
Once the hyaloid artery has firmly tied each lens vesicle to its optic cup, the cup releases its suction-like hold on the lens. As the lens floats out free, its cells and those of the surface of the skin it moves toward become transparent like windows to the outside, to light. At the same time, nerve cell fibers are growing from the base of the optic cup back through the optic stalk to the developing brain (eventually over one million nerve fibers are formed that pass from eye to brain, making the optic stalk into the optic nerve whose transmissions are finally made vision within the brain itself). All the cells in the eye continue to mature until they are capable of responding in concert to light to create the complex of stimuli the optic nerve feeds back to the brain to produce vision.

Studying the history of the eye's growth enabled me to develop a metaphoric model of the activity of "seeing." In each developmental stage, except for the very first one, there is simultaneously both movement outward from the neural core toward the surface periphery of the body and movement inward from the outside toward the neural core. The stages successively provide a more and more complex and elaborate map of precisely how these oppositional streams of moving cells and light waves can travel, grow, and interrelate.

With abstraction, this model of a developing and "seeing" eye can be used as a metaphor for a way in which any cell, cellular organism, or organism segment with a self-enclosed membrane or skin might interact with its environment or world outside it.

If all the stages are put together in a single composite picture, they form a complex but consistent pattern of fluid dynamics. As the core moves outward toward surface, it also expands to cover a broader area. Seeping out past the surface membrane, it dissipates even more widely into space. As the outside moves inward through the surface membrane, it coalesces as if compacting the whole of the boundless outside into a tiny enclosed globe. Concentrating even more, it continues to stream into and through the center of the central core itself. [fig. 4]

This composite model for the inward and outward dynamics of the "seeing" eye allowed me to coach my rigid-eyed students much more effectively in methods by which they could achieve visual mobility. While different aspects of the metaphor would need to be emphasized for each of my two different students, the same metaphor would—with all of its intrinsic balance—be appropriate for both. Nei-

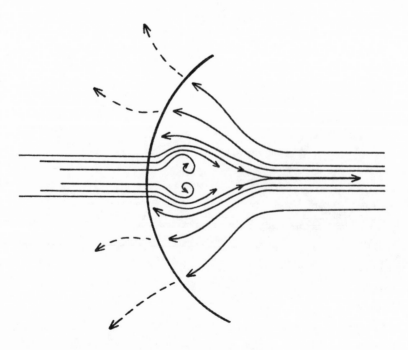

fig. 4—A composite metaphorical model for the dynamics of "seeing."

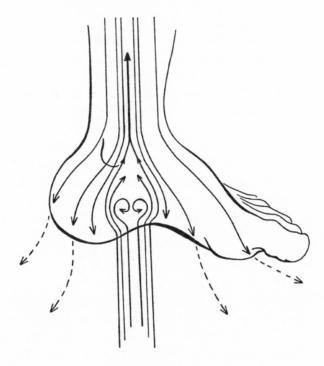

fig. 5—Metaphoric "seeing" with the foot.

ther would have to give up his or her preferred direction of visual movement, but each would simultaneously add to it an interaction with the complementary opposite of that movement.

This fluid-dynamics metaphor that describes "seeing" serves equally well as a model for the pathways of connection between feet and ground in such activities as standing and walking. The sole of each foot functions like a retina that grows developmentally outward from the pelvis, central core structure of the body, down through the leg to spread the bottom surface of the foot in an ever-widening base of support that is "looking" down and out into the ground. The ground itself is visualized as a transparent cornea through which light passes from the living earth beneath. The light enters the foot which receives the light in the curved space beneath its central dome. The light continues to travel up through the dome and into the central axis of the leg, thrusting the bones—like light beams— straight up into the pelvis they support. [fig. 5]

When I verbally suggest to students that they might visualize their feet (or any other parts of themselves) as if these were eyes "seeing" in the way I have just described, I almost always reiterate that suggestion with the touch of my hands. Sometimes I will communicate the fluid dynamics of "seeing" with touch alone. Once this communication has been accomplished, the recipient of the metaphor (who perhaps wishes to be a teacher him or herself) may ask me how I am able to use my fingers in such a magical way. For years, I didn't know an answer. I would blush and shrug my shoulders. I would mumble that I hadn't really done anything and that it was really the student who per-formed his or her own magic. Suddenly, I realized the obvious: my hands could communicate the metaphor of "seeing" by being used as if they themselves were "seeing" eyes.

The entire surface of my palm, including my fingertips, acts like a retina that has grown and is still growing from my brain, along my spinal cord, through my arms, to the skin of my hand. The surface of the skin of the other person is like a transparent cornea through which my retina/hand "looks" to see the space contained within that other person. Within the boundaries of the other person's skin lies a complex and varied landscape, a self-regulating ecosystem composed of interacting bone, muscle, fascia, nerve, blood, organs, and glandu-lar cells. The light that illuminates this landscape and/or the meta-bolic heat produced by all the cellular processes conjoined within the other person's ecosystem all passes through that person's cornea/skin and into my receptive retina/hand. Each sensory nerve cell in my hand that is in contact with the other person's skin is functioning like a rod or cone, transforming the light into optic nerve impulses which continue to travel all the way through the central axis of my arm, back into my spinal cord and into my brain which integrates and turns these impulses into a picture of that other person's body landscape.

The conceptualization of the use of my hand in terms of this metaphor offers explanation not only of how my fingers communi-cate imagery to another person (I concentrate on the idea of the image in the cortex of my brain and this is transmitted via my spinal cord and peripheral nerves to the muscles of my fingers so that they embed the intent of the image into the sensory nerve-filled skin of the other person), but also how my hand monitors the effect of its motor message on the other person so as to ensure that the message is, in fact, received precisely in the desired manner. (I receive with the sensitive nerve endings in the skin of my own fingertips what the other person's motor response to my message is; I actually feel what the movement of his or her bodily ecosystem is in response to my tactilely encoded idea). Then, if the other person has received an idea even slightly different in form or quality from the exact one I had intended, I immediately know this and can adjust my touch until it is conveying just what the other person requires in order to receive the movement I originally envisioned.

Our hands, functioning as if they were eyes, are not limited to transmitting only the idea of "seeing" to the person they touch. An infinite variety of ideas and metaphors can be passed from one per-son to another through touch. The only limitation is that, since the metaphor is given through the passage of movement (from tiny mus-cular movements in the hand of one person to the pressure-sensitive nerve endings in the skin of the other person), the metaphor itself

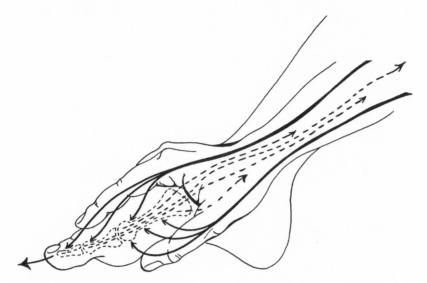

fig. 6—"Seeing" with my hand.

must be a dynamic one, that is, a metaphor about the pathways that energy expenditure takes through space and time. In order to actually succeed at communicating a dynamic metaphor to someone else, I myself must keep its motion etched with crystalline clarity in my own mind.[fig. 6]

That the metaphor I transmit will develop and change is inevitable, as evidenced in this article. My metaphor for "seeing" evolved considerably in the very process of describing it and then applying it here. In clarifying, and therefore specifying and elaborating the metaphor, I was led to perceive how that metaphor provides one kind of descriptive model for communicating through touch.

I use my hands as much as I use my eyes when teaching movement to another person. It takes, therefore, only a small step to conjoin the activities of touching and seeing into the same metaphoric vehicle. However, any step is movement into the unknown. In striding out, the landscape around me will surely change into one that is strange and mysterious. The metaphor I carry with me may serve as a beam of light into this new land, but all else will be shadow. New metaphors will have to follow if the whole environment is to be illuminated.

10

Metaphors of Touch

W hen I touch someone, that person touches me back. There is simultaneous and immediate communication of movement between us. Having already written at great length about the kinds of movement communications I often make to others with my own hands and why, I write here about movement communications received with my hands from other people.

In order to sensitively receive that communication, I need to keep myself in a state of lucid "neutrality": mechanically balanced, emotionally calm, mentally open and without any urgency to succeed. Otherwise, my own internal activities function as a kind of "white noise" that interferes with my ability to perceive the person I am touching.

While maintaining a state of lucid neutrality, it is possible to feel contrast and variations in such features as form, temperature, texture, density, viscosity, rhythms, and rate of motion as I carefully move my fingers over another person's skin to feel what underlies that surface membrane. Over the years I have come to understand each of the different body systems as having its own distinctive combinations of characteristics that I can feel with my fingers. I often describe my tactile perception of these characteristics with metaphors. Here are some of the metaphors I associate with the systems of skin, fascia, muscles, bones and joints, the movement of blood and lymph, organs and glands, and the nervous system.

The exploration of skin with my fingers is like a pursuit of topography, the study of surfaces. Our skin both separates and connects our inner and outer worlds. Our skin contains many nerve endings and is therefore extremely responsive to touch. Some of the skin receptors trigger responses in the deeper layers of our body, such as underlying muscles and even organs (conversely, an unusual skin response is sometimes being referred from a deeper source).

Fascia, the body's connective tissue, can be easily thought of as the "skin" for the internal body structures. However, this characterization does not suggest the awesome prevalence of fascia in the body. Not only is every structure in the body encased in fascia; but fascia also separates and links each structure of the body from and to every other, making its surfaces many-layered and convoluted. If you ever wondered what it is that connects and pulls from your big toe to your ear when you do an extravagant full-body stretch, the answer is: fascia. The fascia that forms a full-body stocking just under our skin is our superficial fascia (especially thick in our low back and outer thigh regions). There are multiple layers beneath that, all the way to the specialized fascia, called dura, which surrounds our body core, i.e., our spinal cord and brain.

Exploring fascia through touch, we can continue to use a topographic model, but we must think of many surfaces layered on top of each other (like mille-feuille pastry or the layers of rock and sand that form the earth's crust). Fascia is elastic, but not as soft as skin. Each layer of fascia has its own directional pull along which it will stretch more or less easily, not unlike woven fabric. Since it surrounds muscle, lengthening a muscle also lengthens fascia. However, muscle is "smart"—it has innervation to permit it to actively and intentionally contract or not. Fascia, in contrast, is "dumb"—it has no motor innervation—therefore, the length and surface shape of fascia can only be altered passively through movement imposed by forces other than its own.

One can think of the ubiquitous fascia as the historical record of the body, since its present condition reflects movement and positions assumed by the surrounding structures in the past. For example, long-term shortening in the erector spinae muscles of the lower back results in a shortening of the surrounding fascia. Subsequently, a swayback posture is maintained by the lumbar fascia even after the supporting lower back muscles are elongated by a program of conscious releasing and stretching.[fig. 1]

Our muscles, encased and surrounded by fascia, can be perceived as the "engines" responsible for producing the movement of our bony levers through space. Muscles can only pull on bones, never push. If the skin and fascia are analogous to the topography of the earth, then the muscles are analogous to the earth's geology.

Muscles have depth and volume as well as surface. As mentioned before, a highly significant difference between muscle and

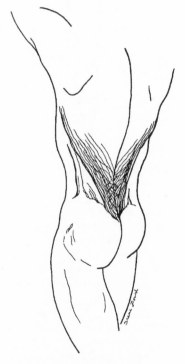

fig. 1— This is a view of the most superficial layer of the lumbar fascia that connects the back of the pelvis with the back of the rib cage. If it is shortened, it contributes to lumbar lordosis, or "swayback."

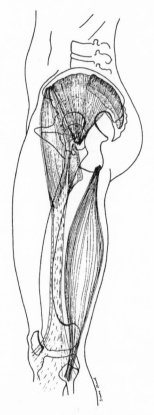

fig. 2—A side view of the pelvis and thigh. The gluteus maximus is cut away to more clearly reveal the underlying muscles. When a person thinks of shifting his or her weight to one side, or actually shifts the weight, the tensor fascia lata, gluteus medius, gluteus minimus, and the lateral hamstring become more active on that side. By touching the outside of the pelvis, one can easily feel the bulge of the tensor fascia lata and the gluteus medius as they "harden" in anticipation of an imagined weight shift.

fascia is that muscle is "smart"; that is, it is innervated by motor nerves. This means we can voluntarily direct the activity of a muscle and therefore affect its shape. Because it is "smart," muscle can be altered by the application of ideas or images. Suppose someone is standing with weight evenly distributed over both legs. If that person simply imagines shifting his or her pelvis to the left, I will be able to feel some change in the activity of the muscles on the outside of the person's left hip. These muscles will ripple under the skin, bulge outward slightly towards my fingers, and feel a bit harder to my touch. When the person changes his or her mind, imagining a weight shift onto the right foot, I will be able to feel change in the muscles which I am still touching. Now, the muscles on the outside of the left hip will indent under my fingers and will feel a little softer to my touch. If I place my fingers on the outsides of both of the person's hips, I will be able to tell if he or she is imagining standing on the right or on the left, even if the person doesn't visibly move. The muscles will bulge more firmly into my fingers on the side the person imagines standing on, while the muscles on the side he or she imagines shifting away from will indent under my fingers.[fig. 2]

I consider the movement of bones as being like the movement of planets in a miniature solar system, a series of minutely but infinitely varied orbital pathways. Our bones are levers whose relative stiffness allows us to carry the mass of our body directionally through space. All bones are spiral in form. It is in the joints between the bones where the actual movement takes place. Through touch and observation, I can both locate the joint line at which the movement takes place and identify restrictions to that motion by noticing the range and quality of motion at that joint. If the joint moves very smoothly and then stops with a solid distinct end-feel, then I know that I am feeling the position at which the two articulating bones have run into each other. There is no longer room to move because the ligaments that hold that joint together are fully taut and the joint surfaces of each bone have been fully traversed. If the joint stops moving with a slightly resilient or springy end-feel, then I know I am feeling the limitation to motion imposed by the length of fascia or the activity of muscles.

Each joint has different potential ranges of motion due to the shape of the articulating joint surfaces and the state of the surrounding soft tissues such as the ligaments and muscles. All joint surfaces, however, are rounded, one surface being concave and the other convex. Therefore, movement at any joint describes an arc through space. There are no straight lines in this realm. If I follow the motion of a bony joint with my fingers, I follow curved joint surfaces and spherical space through which the spiral-shaped bones orbit, imagining myself to be an astronomer.[fig. 3]

One can describe the movement characteristics of skin, fascia,

fig. 3— Illustration of the hip joint. The hip socket (acetabulum) in the pelvis is concave and the head of the femur is convex. The femur can "orbit" around the hip socket in all dimensions.

muscles, and bones primarily in terms of their spatial qualities; e.g., their changes in size, shape, direction, arcs of movement, etc. When focusing on the movement of the fluid circulatory systems of the body, it is essential to attend to the temporal aspects of the movement as well.

As I "listen" to the flow patterns of these fluids, I can describe their contrasting qualities. The pattern of flow through the blood vessels is like the progression of water down a stream that is pumped at one end. In contrast, lymph flows viscously and irregularly, perhaps like the colloidal suspension of sand and water that forms the muddy bed of a swamp. These fluid systems can be studied in terms of the complex and elegant physics of fluid dynamics.

Blood is the easiest fluid to monitor. I can directly feel the pulse of arterial flow by touching the front of someone's wrist, for example. Arterial blood is pumped rhythmically by the heart through the arteries whose strongly binding elasticity does not allow the heart's pulse to diffuse. Venous blood is pumped back through the thinner-walled veins by movement produced from the alternate contraction and relaxation of muscles and concomitant motion of joints. Arteries are firmer than veins. They are easily felt to have the characteristic rhythmic pulse impelled by the heartbeat.

Veins are more malleable than arteries, and their irregular motion is a function of the many forces acting on them to propel the returning blood through one-way valves back to the heart. These forces include the elastic properties of the veins themselves, the elastic quality of the surrounding tissues, the activity of the surrounding muscles, and even the elastic properties of clothing and other externals, such as gravity or the touch of another's hands.

The lymphatic system can be thought of as an auxiliary to venous return. Lymph flow is from the periphery of the body to the center, in the same direction as venous flow. The lymph system monitors, filters, and returns to the heart cellular fluids not carried by the veins, with the addition of dead white cells and other immune system sentinels and fighters. It is not pumped by the heart but is instead propelled only by the action of the muscles and organs around it. Since its main, central deep-level channel travels along the front of the thoracic spine, the pumping produced by breathing is itself a prime mover of lymph in its final progression back to the heart. Lymph's viscosity, speed, and rhythm are determined by the state of the immune system, cellular health, breathing, and level of the body's physical activity at the moment.

The superficial lymphatic vessels enter nodes at the joints: very large ones at armpit, base of neck, and groin areas, moderately large ones at elbows, knees, wrists, and ankles. These are quite easy to feel with your fingers when there is a local infection, such as a mosquito bite. Even in the absence of any congestion, it is easy to find the relatively large lymph nodes at the groin in front of the hip.

Just as blood may be perceived as moving quickly, lymph is a more primitive and slower system. Where arterial blood flow is clearly metered, venous and lymphatic movement is not metered at all. While arterial blood is like a pulsing river, lymph can seem like a peat bog by comparison.

It is possible to feel the effects of venous and lymphatic pooling due to a sluggish return of these fluids to the heart. Perhaps after the person I am touching has been sitting for a long car trip, that person's feet will feel warm and distended. I might actually see that person's feet appear red or mottled. The tops of the shoes may be marked deeply into the skin. If the person has raised his or her feet for me to examine them, they will soon feel more normal just from the effect of being elevated and moved by my fingers.

If the person sat with one foot folded under him or her during that long car trip, then the person has not only compromised fluid return to the heart, but also compromised arterial outflow and nerve signals to the foot as a result of pressure. In this case, the foot will feel cool and not responsive at all to my touch for a few moments. If I continue to lightly stroke the foot with the tips of my fingers, its surface will quickly warm and become responsive and even hypersensitive, like the whiskers on a cat. The person might exclaim that he or she feels sensations of "pinpricks" or "fire ants" at the same time that my fingers feel more normal blood flow in his or her feet.

One may begin to sense and understand the motion of organ and glandular systems in terms of very long temporal phrases that last for many hours, days, or even years. These lengthy choreographies are always in relation with or contrast to each other.

Glands are characterized by their ability to secrete a substance that can be carried (usually via the circulatory system) to other locations in the body. Organs are characterized by their specialized ability to carry out a function that alters or processes substances that pass through them.

Any variation in the amount and/or type of secretion produced by a particular gland can have effects on each and all the other body systems in elaborate ways. Any shift in the processing capacities of a particular organ can likewise result in adjustments and changes within all the other body systems. Increased activity in one organ or gland can produce decrease in its antagonist organ or gland, and vice versa. Thus, my fingers may very well feel contrasts between the activities of different organs. For example, when I feel someone's lungs to be very active because that person has just been running for a while, I will probably feel that person's stomach to be minimally active because it will have long-since emptied itself of any digesting food.

Generally, when an organ or gland is healthy, it is so fluid and adaptable to my touching fingers that I may have difficulty distinguishing it from its surrounding neighbors. A healthy thyroid gland (snuggled around the Adam's apple or thyroid cartilage), for example, can barely be palpated when it moves up and down along with the Adam's apple in swallowing. The thyroid usually feels like a light padding on either side of the cartilage. However, when it is inflamed (as in thyroiditis) it will feel hotter than the surrounding area. When it is enlarged (as in goiter), it can be felt as a distinctive bulging mass.

When touching to perceive the state of the organ and glandular systems, I think of myself as an oceanographer. As such, I can feel the tides and surface currents that are determined by both global or internal influences, such as deep ocean streams or temperature differentials, and celestial or external influences, such as the phase of the moon or a solar flare. Organs, like the stomach, also move as a function of internal body influences, such as hunger, and external influences, such as the availability and subsequent consumption of a piece of chocolate. It is also possible to submerge myself deep within the inner recesses of the body by gently and obliquely directing my fingertips downward and inward. From my "submarine," I can perceive the creatures that move there and the ecology near the ocean floor in which they live. These volcanoes, deep valleys, and seaweed forests are never fully illuminated by sunlight. If I move ever so slowly and carefully over time, exploring a little more each time I "submerge," I can eventually feel patterns of motion pertaining to each organ residing in the fluid realm of the abdominal cavity, for example, despite the lack of well-lit pathways.

The nervous system can be perceived by my fingers in the way that the wind can be perceived by my eyes: only indirectly. I see the tree branches moving to the south, but not the north wind that blows them in that direction. Since the nervous system initiates, coordinates, and stimulates all body systems, I know it by the activity it produces in those same body systems. Without it, no system moves at all. If the nervous system is less than fully functional, the patterns of interactions of all the other systems are chaotic or disharmonious. The nervous system, in my metaphoric cosmology, is an enormous symphony with a brilliant conductor who is able to direct each instrumentalist simultaneously and exquisitely. The movement of signals along nerves is so rapid as to seem instantaneous. This gives us the satisfying illusion that our brain and any particular cell in the periphery (say, a muscle cell in the index finger) are in simultaneous synchrony. In fact, studies have shown that they are not. Many milliseconds pass between the time our eye sees a flash of light and our brain sends an impulse to our finger to move so that it presses a button.

It is possible to touch and identify the large sciatic nerve with my fingers, for example, if I feel for it in the region between the sitting bone (tuberosity of the ischium) and the outside of the hip (greater trochanter of the femur). It will feel like a thick round cord. Normally, unless it is inflamed, the person being touched does not feel the nerve itself, but only the results of its transmissions. One feels sensations, such as temperature, pressure, pain, and itch due to transmissions from the periphery *to* the spinal cord and brain. In contrast, one produces movements of the bones through space due to transmissions to the muscles *from* the brain and spinal cord.

Nerves transmit impulses via electric currents. These currents are themselves affected and altered in terms of intensity, speed, duration, and spatial pathways, by continuous changes in production by the brain of specialized chemicals called neurotransmitters. The relative concentration of these chemicals at any given site within the nervous system at a particular moment is contingent on such factors as previous experience (that is, learning), level of alertness, fatigue, metabolism, and emotional and hormonal states, as well as the amount and type of stimulus being received by the brain at that moment.

Even the simplest neurological response involves millions of nerve synapses (connections between nerves across which impulses are transmitted). Any action can be thought of as a vast orchestral performance or temporal-spatial web of interactions within the nervous system. There are many different instruments in the orchestra, and each one plays its score of different tones in various sequences through time, but the music is the summation of all the instruments playing together. When I am attending to the nervous system, I like to imagine that I am listening to a symphony in which each and every cell of the body is a player.

My experience of the different body systems can be summarized in metaphors. I sense skin and fascia as surface — topography. I perceive muscle as having depth and volume — geology. Skeletal joints are characterized by orbital movement — astronomy. The fluid systems of blood and lymph are identified by the rate and rhythm of their directional linear flow — fluid dynamics of rivers, streams, and bogs. The glandular and organ systems are perceivable as moving in elaborate patterns of confluent function throughout the body, generated over long diurnal cycles and biorhythms — oceanography. I run at fast forward through my memory before I can fully sense them. I begin to comprehend the complex web patterns of the nervous system if I think orchestrally — music of the galaxies.

The kinds of things that I "hear" skin and fascia telling me are about elasticity and extensibility (or restriction). Muscle tells me about extensibility as well as contractility. Joints inform me about their surrounding muscles and also about their intrinsic mobility (or stiffness). Fluid systems talk about rhythm (or arrhythmia), speed, dilation (or constriction) of the vessels which carry the fluids, viscosity and congestion. The glandular and organ systems talk about resilience (or rigidity), adaptability, and long-term complex interactions. The nervous system tells me indirectly, but clearly, about communication channels, syntheses and networks of functional control. In reality, all communication by and from the various body systems is enacted by the nervous system of the person I am touching as well as by my own.

Generally, I perceive a system to be at ease when there is vitality, rhythmic variation, and harmony. I perceive a system to be under duress when it resists movement, is distinctly hot or cold, rapid or slow, arrhythmic or utterly still. In other words, if a particular structure seems to be moving in an aberrant or dissonant fashion, then I pay very careful attention to what it has to communicate to me. I may learn something new and important.

To perceive each system of the body through touch, I convey vectors of motion to, from, and around all the structures of each system as if I were using sonar to search within the entire body. The movement I convey through my hands initiates a kind of kinesthetic conversation with the various tissues of the person I am touching. As I move responsively I begin to understand what a particular group of cells is conveying to me. Eventually, the person I am touching creates more sustained, complex, and varied choreographies for the motion of his or her cells, as a function of having become more aware of existing and alternative patterns. It is as if the person creates a more spacious and ecologically rich inner land to move through. This happens by the very process of traveling through the rainforests and deserts, the mountains and ocean beds, as well as the superhighways of the person's own inner realm of physical being.

Annotated
Bibliography

Arey, Leslie B. *Developmental Anatomy,* revised seventh edition. Philadelphia: W. B. Saunders, 1974. This text was one of the resources for my metaphoric model of the development of the eye.

Basmajian, John and Deluca, Carlo J. *Muscles Alive: Their Functions Revealed by Electromyography,* fifth edition. Baltimore: Williams and Wilkins, 1985. Basmajian did some of the first studies of actual (not just theoretical) muscle activity involved during walking, breathing, etc.

Brooks, Vernon B. *The Neural Basis of Motor Control.* New York: Oxford University Press, 1986. In this book many of my suspicions about motor learning were given support while many of my areas of ignorance were greatly illuminated.

Carr, Janet H. and Shepherd, Roberta B. *A Motor Relearning Programme for Stroke.* Rockville, Md.: Aspen Systems Corp., 1987. This practical down-to-earth and intrinsically optimistic approach to relearning after a major insult to the nervous system is precise, and consonant with my own.

Chatwin, Bruce. *The Songlines.* New York: Penguin Books, 1987. Reading this book about the Australian aborigine relationship to the lived-in world helped me articulate some of my own experience of creating space within the body of the person I am touching. Although I do not know enough to determine the accuracy of Chatwin's assessment of the aborigine mind, the ideas engendered in my mind while reading Chatwin's book were intensely stimulating to my own creations.

Cheng Man-ch'ing and Smith, Robert W. *T'ai-Chi: The "Supreme Ultimate" Exercise for Health, Sport, and Self-Defense.* Rutland, Vermont: Charles E. Tuttle Co., 1967. This is the book of my late mentor in tai chi chuan. What I know about this martial art comes mostly from him and his students, especially Lou Kleinsmith and Margaret Newman.

Granit, Ragnar. *The Purposive Brain.* Boston: MIT Press, 1977. This lucid writing on an enormously complex subject assisted me while preparing my first lectures in 1979 on the role of the nervous system in directional goal-oriented movement. Despite advances in the neurosciences, this slim volume still provides important ways of organizing one's field of inquiry, especially with reference to purpose, causality, or intentionality of the nervous system.

Hoppenfeld, Stanley. *Physical Examination of the Spine and Extremities.* New York: Appleton-Century-Crofts, 1976. Hoppenfeld's charming drawings show the surface landmarks of the body that direct the examiner to the underlying musculoskeletal and neurological structures.

Inman, Verne T., Ralston, Henry J., and Todd, Frank. *Human Walking.* Baltimore: Williams and Wilkins, 1981. This book illustrates some of the elaborate joint and muscle interactions that can be involved in the human gait.

Kahle, Werner, Leonhardt, Helmut, and Platzer, Werner. *Color Atlas and Textbook of Human Anatomy.* Chicago: Year Book Medical Publishers, 1979. Three volumes —*Locomotor System, Internal Organs,* and *Nervous System and Sensory Organs*— are in easy-to-use paper-back books that offer an enormous amount of information about the body systems.

Kapandji, I. A. *The Physiology of the Joints.* London: Churchill Livingstone, 1970. Three volumes of superb kinetic illustrations of how joints move and are moved by muscles.

Karp, Theodore. *Dictionary of Music.* New York: Dell, 1973. The musical terminology defined in this book is almost always directly applicable to movement and the teaching of movement through voice and touch.

Keller, Evelyn F. *A Feeling for the Organism: The Life and Work of Barbara McClintock.* New York: W. H. Freeman and Company, 1983. Barbara McClintock's descriptions of how she perceived the genetic processes taking place inside corn cells, eventually leading her to transform the whole science of genetics, were inspirational for me. They gave me the courage to continue describing my own kind of "cellular" perceptions of the human body.

Kendall, Florence P., McCreary, Elizabeth K., and Provance, Patricia G. *Muscles: Testing and Function,* fourth edition. Baltimore: Williams and Wilkins, 1993. Photographs and drawings illustrate testing of each of the skeletal muscles for function both in posture and motion.

Kleinman, Arthur. *The Illness Narratives: Suffering, Healing and the Human Condition.* New York: Basic Books, 1988. Kleinman looks at illness and mortality from an anthropological and medical viewpoint. His observation that people feel a need to create meaning out of their life experience is consistent with my own.

Luria, Aleksandr R. *Cognitive Development: Its Cultural and Social Foundations.* Cambridge, Ma.: Harvard University Press, 1976. This great Russian neuropsychologist has written many books that have been important to my own understanding of cognition. In this book he talks about the concrete thinking engaged in by preliterate peasants. I find this kind of thinking operating frequently in people who refer to their own physical being as "the body," rather than "my body."

Pansky, Ben and Delmas, J. A. *Review of Neuroscience*. New York: Macmillan, 1980. The illustrations in this book provided understandings that informed my own drawings and descriptions of the development of the human eye.

Pernkopf, Eduard. *Atlas of Topographical and Applied Human Anatomy*. Philadelphia: W. B. Saunders, 1963. These two volumes include very fine color illustrations of the vascular, nervous, organ systems, and musculoskeletal systems.

Sacks, Oliver. *A Leg to Stand On*. New York: Harper and Row, 1984. This book describes a neurologist's own subjective experience with a serious injury. He gives a rather impassioned plea for more subjective description of trauma from the point of view of the person suffering it. This encouraged me to pursue my own subjective studies and helped me articulate the difference between a subjective or internal view and an objective or external view of human movement.

Seashore, Carl E. *Psychology of Music*. New York: McGraw-Hill, 1938. A classic book that addresses the relationship between sound and musical perception. Reading this book helped me articulate my own concepts about the relationship between movement sensations and the interpretation of this data as perception.

Smith, Judith A. *The Idea of Health: Implications for the Nursing Professional*. New York: Teachers College, Columbia University, 1983. This book, along with many personal conversations with the author, assisted me in comprehending some of the special ideas my students have about the nature of physical well-being and health.

Sweigard, Lulu E. *Human Movement Potential: Its Ideokinetic Facilitation*. New York: Harper and Row, 1974. This is the book written by my mentor to elucidate her use of imagery. She wrote it during the time when I was her assistant at the Juilliard School. Her role in my professional life was enormous.

Todd, Mabel. *The Thinking Body*. New York: Dance Horizons, 1937. Todd was the mentor of my mentor, Lulu E. Sweigard. Todd's writing is both exquisite and playful. The origin of Sweigard's and therefore my own work in neuromuscular retraining is in this book.

Trungpa, Chogyam. *Cutting Through Spiritual Materialism*. Boston: Shambhala Publications, 1973. This book helped me come to terms with the limitations and the responsibilities of my role as a teacher.

Wall, Patrick D. and Melzack, Ronald, editors. *Textbook of Pain,* third edition. London: Churchill Livingstone, 1994. This gigantic volume includes research and theory about almost every conceivable aspect of that scourge and mystery, pain. It serves as a significant reminder that we never "know" ourselves fully.

Wessells, Norman K., editor. *Vertebrate Structures and Functions*. San Francisco: Scientific American, W. H. Freeman and Company, 1974. The articles by Napier, "The Antiquity of Human Walking" and "The Evolution of the Hand," were of particular interest to me.

Biographical Note

IRENE DOWD has a B.A. in philosophy from Vassar College, studied anatomy and neuroanatomy at Columbia-Presbyterian Medical School, and neuroscience at Teachers College, Columbia University. She studied with and assisted Dr. Lulu E. Sweigard at the Juilliard School from 1968 through 1974. Her own choreography has been strongly influenced by her study of dance with a number of choreographers, especially Merce Cunningham, Lucas Hoving, Antony Tudor, José Limón, and Viola Farber. Since 1970 she has taught dance, dance composition, functional and kinesthetic anatomy at such institutions as Teachers College, Columbia University, Wesleyan University, the Juilliard School, the American Dance Festival, the Naropa Institute, the Laban/Bartenieff Institute for Movement Studies, and the National Ballet School of Canada. From 1984 to 1986, Irene was co-principal investigator in a study on "Effects of Neuromuscular Retraining on Mobility of the Elderly," with Judith A. Smith, Ph.D., R.N., as principal investigator, funded by the Center for Nursing Research at the University of Pennsylvania. She has maintained a private practice in neuromuscular training for over thirty years. Her words and drawings have appeared in *Eddy, Dance Scope, Contact Quarterly, Dance Research Journal of CORD, Pour La Danse, La Danza, Dance Magazine,* and *Schmerz und Sports (Pain in Sports: Interdisciplinary Paintherapy in Sportsmedicine).*